Air Fryer Cookbook

1000 Day Air Fryer Recipes for Your Family

By Ashley Randolph

Copyright© 2018 by Ashley Randolph

All rights reserved

This document is geared towards providing exact and reliable information in regards to the topic and issue covered. The publication is sold with the idea that the publisher is not required to render accounting, officially permitted, or otherwise, qualified services. If advice is necessary, legal or professional, a practiced individual in the profession should be ordered.

From a declaration of principles which was accepted and approved equally by a committee of the American bar association and a committee of publishers and associations.

Legal Declaim

In no way is it legal to reproduce, duplicate, or transmit any part of this document in either electronic means or in printed format. Recording of this publication is strictly prohibited and any storage of this document is not allowed unless with written permission from the publisher.

The information provided herein is stated to be truthful and consistent, in that any liability, in terms of inattention or otherwise, by any usage or abuse of any policies, processes, or directions contained within is the solitary and utter responsibility of the recipient reader. Under no circumstances will any legal responsibility or blame be held against the publisher for any reparation, damages, or monetary loss due to the information herein, either directly or indirectly.

Table of Content

Introduction	1
Chapter 1 Go to Air Fryer	2
Air Fryer Benefits	4
Useful Tips	5
Safeguards	5
Air Fryer Cooking Charts	7
1000 Days Meal Plan for Air Fryer	8
Chapter 2 Air Fryer Recipes	9
Breakfast Recipes	10
Creamy Broccoli Egg Scramble	10
Loaded Breakfast Hash Browns	11
Breakfast Biscuits, Eggs 'n Bacon	11
Hash Brown, Sausage 'n Cauliflower Bake	12
Cauliflower-Broccoli Egg Bake	12
Raisin 'n Apple French Toast	13
Overnight French Toast with Blueberries	13
Eggs Benedict in an Overnight Casserole	14
Egg-Substitute 'n Bacon Casserole	14
Country style Brekky Casserole	15
Amish Style Brekky Casserole	15
Baked Cornbread and Eggs	16
Feta and Spinach Brekky Pie	16
Cheesy-Bacon Casserole	17
Mixed Vegetable Frittata	17
Breakfast Chicken Casserole	18
Rice Casserole Mexican Style	18
Broccoli, Ham 'n Potato Casserole	19
Cheeseburger and Bacon Casserole	19
Main Meal Recipes	20
Turkey 'n Broccoli Bake	20
Penne Chicken Pesto Bake	21
Green Bean Chicken Stuffing Bake	21
Cheesy Broccoli-Rice Bake	22
Rice Casserole Mexican Style	22
Mouth-Watering Taco Bake	23
A Different Rice-Chik'n Bake	23
Chicken Florentine Bake	24
Sea Scallop Bake	24
Shrimp Casserole Louisiana Style	25
Cheesy Zucchini-Squash Bake	25
Portuguese Bacalao Tapas	26
Zucchini & Carrot Bake	26
Cheesy-Creamy Broccoli Bake	27
Mushroom 'n Spinach Casserole	27
Potato Casserole Twice Baked	28
Chili Rellenos Bake	28
Spicy Zucchini Bake Mexican Style	29
Feta-Spinach 'n Pita Casserole	29
Chicken Deluxe Tetrazzini	30
Nutritious Cabbage Roll Bake	30
Vegan Approved Shepherd's Pie	31
Enchilada Leftovers Casserole	31
Rice, Chicken 'n Salsa Casserole	33
Veggie-Pasta 'n chicken Bake	33
Yummy Mac 'n Cheese	34
Black Bean and Brown Rice Bake	35
Herb and Zucchini Bake	35
Lobster Lasagna Maine Style	36

Rice and Tuna Puff	37
Yellow Squash Bake, Low Carb	37
Eggplant-Parm Bake	38
Seven Layers of Tortilla Pie	39
Penne Pasta 'n Portobello Bake	39
Southwest Style Meaty Casserole	40
Easy-Bake Spanish Rice	41
Brown Rice 'n Chicken Curry Casserole	41

Grilled Poultry Recipes 42

Rotisserie Chicken with Herbes De Provence	42
Grilled Oregano Chicken	42
Honey Sriracha Chicken	43
Tequila Glazed Chicken	43
Grilled Sambal Chicken	44
Smoked Chicken Wings	44
Sweet and Sour Grilled Chicken	45
Lemon Grilled Chicken Breasts	45
Spicy Peach Glazed Grilled Chicken	46
Chinese Style Chicken	46
Garlic Cilantro-Lime Chicken	47
Grilled Chicken Stuffed with Cheese	47
Southwest Chicken Foil Packets	48
Teriyaki Grilled Chicken	48
Sweet and Spicy Grilled Chicken	49
Hone, Lime, And Lime Grilled Chicken	49
Grilled Jerk Chicken	50
Butterflied Chicken with Herbs	50
4-Ingredient Garlic Herb Chicken Wings	51
Pesto Grilled Chicken	51
Chili and Yogurt Marinated Chicken	52
Grilled Chicken with Board Dressing	52
Indian Spiced Chicken Eggplant and Tomato Skewers	53
Easy Curry Grilled Chicken Wings	53
Spicy Chicken with Lemon and Parsley in A Packet	54
Korean Grilled Chicken	54
Grilled Chicken with Shishito Peppers	55
Grilled Chicken with Scallions	55
Piri Piri Chicken	56
Grilled Turmeric and Lemongrass Chicken	56
Peruvian Grilled Chicken	57
Air Fryer Grilled Moroccan Chicken	57
Rotisserie Chicken with Herbes De Provence	58
Grilled Oregano Chicken	58
Honey Sriracha Chicken	59
Tequila Glazed Chicken	59
Grilled Sambal Chicken	60
Smoked Chicken Wings	60
Sweet and Sour Grilled Chicken	61
Lemon Grilled Chicken Breasts	61
Spicy Peach Glazed Grilled Chicken	62
Chinese Style Chicken	62

Vegetable Recipes 63

Air Fried Grilled Asparagus	63
Grilled Hasselback Potatoes	63
Air Fryer Roasted Vegetables	63
Air Fried Roasted Summer Squash	64
Grilled Cauliflower Bites	64
Roasted Air Fried Vegetables	65
Air Fryer Grilled Mexican Corn	65

Crispy and Spicy Grilled Broccoli in Air Fryer	66
Easy Grilled Corn in The Air Fryer	66
Grilled Pineapple and Peppers	66
Grilled Onion Potatoes	67
Grilled Frozen Vegetables	67
Simple Grilled Vegetables	67
Italian Grilled Vegetables	68
Balsamic Grilled Vegetables	68
Grilled Vegetables with Lemon Herb Vinaigrette	69
Grilled Zucchini with Mozzarella	69
Grilled Vegetables with Garlic	70
Grilled Tomato Melts	70
Asparagus with Hollandaise Sauce	71
Air Fryer Grilled Mushrooms	71
Grilled Asparagus and Arugula Salad	72
Spicy Thai –Style Veggies	72
Grilled Vegetables with Smokey Mustard Sauce	73
Indian Grilled Vegetables	73
Grilled Sweet Potato Wedges with Dipping Sauce	74
Grilled Green Beans with Shallots	74
Grille Tomatoes with Garden Herb Salad	75
Grilled Potato Packets	75
Sweet Onions	76
Roasted Dill Potato Medley	76
Grilled Squash	77
Air Fryer Grilled Fennel	77
Grilled Corn Kabobs	78
Grill Smoked Mushrooms	78

Seafood Recipe	**79**
Blackened Shrimps in Air Fryer	79
Herb and Garlic Fish Fingers	79
Garlic and Black Pepper Shrimp Grill	80
Crispy Cod Nuggets with Tartar Sauce	80
Grilled Salmon with Cucumbers	81
Shrimps, Zucchini, And Tomatoes on the Grill	81
Grilled Halibut with Tomatoes and Hearts of Palm	82
Chat Masala Grilled Snapper	82
One-Pan Shrimp and Chorizo Mix Grill	83
Grilled Tasty Scallops	83
Clam with Lemons on the Grill	84
Salmon Steak Grilled with Cilantro Garlic Sauce	84
Tasty Grilled Red Mullet	85
Chargrilled Halibut Niçoise With Vegetables	85
Spiced Salmon Kebabs	86
Roasted Tuna on Linguine	86
Chili Lime Clams with Tomatoes	87
Air Fryer Garlicky-Grilled Turbot	87
Broiled Spiced-Lemon Squid	88
Tuna Grill with Ginger Sauce	88
Char-Grilled Spicy Halibut	89
Roasted Swordfish with Charred Leeks	89
Citrusy Branzini on the Grill	90
Grilled Squid Rings with Kale and Tomatoes	90
Grilled Shrimp with Butter	91
Char-Grilled 'n Herbed Sea Scallops	91
Japanese Citrus Soy Squid	92

Greek-Style Grilled Scallops	92
Easy Grilled Pesto Scallops	93
Clams with Herbed Butter in Packets	93
Simple Sesame Squid on the Grill	94
Grilled Shellfish with Vegetables	94

Grilled Meat Recipes 95

Skirt Steak with Mojo Marinade	95
Dijon-Marinated Skirt Steak	95
Grilled Carne Asada Steak	96
Chimichurri-Style Steak	96
Strip Steak with Cucumber Yogurt Sauce	97
Grilled BBQ Sausages	97
Medium Rare Simple Salt and Pepper Steak	98
Pounded Flank Steak with Tomato Salsa	98
Strip Steak with Japanese Dipping Sauce	99
Chi Spacca's Bistecca	99
Grilled Steak with Parsley Salad	100
Korean Grilled Skirt Steak	100
Onion Marinated Skirt Steak	101
Grilled Beef Steak with Herby Marinade	101

Dessert & Snacks Recipes 102

Crunchy Crisped Peaches	102
Sour Cream-Blueberry Coffee Cake	102
Five-Cheese Pull Apart Bread	103
Buttery Dinner Rolls	103
Yummy Carrot Cake	104
Delightful Caramel Cheesecake	104
Tangy Orange-Choco cake	105
Amazing with Every Bite Fried Bananas	105
Blackberry-Goodness Cobbler	106
Appetizing Apple Pound Cake	106
Sugared Doughs with Choco Dip	107
Appealingly Coconut-y Cake	107
Cranberry Bread Pudding	108
Luscious Strawberry Cobbler	108
Air Fryed Churros with Choco Dip	109
Out-of-this-World PB&J Doughnuts	109
Enchanting Coffee-Apple Cake	110
Pumpkin Pie in Air Fryer	111
Easy 'n Delicious Brownies	111

Skewer Recipes 112

Chicken and Pineapple BBQ	112
Sweetly Honeyed Chicken Kebabs	112
Skewered Beef Asian Way	113
Teriyaki 'n Hawaiian Chicken	113
Chicken Kebabs Greek Way	114
Skewered Oriental Teriyaki Beef	114
Grilled Beef with Ginger-Hoisin	115
Spiced Lime 'n Coconut Shrimp Skewer	115
Tangy Grilled Fig-Prosciutto	116
Veggie Souvlaki on Air Fryer Grill	116
Swordfish with Sage on the Grill	116
Scallops and Bacon Grill	117
Grilled Chipotle Shrimp	117
Grilled Chicken Shish Tanoak	118
Beef Eastern Shish Kebabs	118
Dill-Rubbed Grilled Salmon	119
Turkey Meatballs in Skewer	119

Grilled Curried Chicken	120
Cajun Pork on the Grill	120
Peppered & Carbonated Sirloin Kebabs	121
Grilled Jerk Chicken	121
Chicken Caesar on the Grill	122
Rosemary-Rubbed Grilled Lamb	122
Thai-Style Grilled Pork	123
Hungarian Style Grilled Beef	123
Grilled Buccaneer Pork	124
Grilled Steak with Scallion Dip	124

Baked Recipes 126

Orange-Caesar Dressed Roughie	126
Salmon with Crisped Topped Crumbs	126
Orange & Tofu Fry	127
Gouda-Spinach Stuffed Pork	128
Scrumptious Shrimp Scampi Fry	128
Baked Cod in Air Fryer	129
Tender Chicken Thigh Bake	129
Chicken Teriyaki Bake	130
Meatball Pizza Bake	130
Pepperoni Calzone Bake	131
Comforting Beef Stew Bake	131
Roll-up Chicken Reuben	132
Chicken Mediterranean Fry	132
Crusted Fish with Dijon	133
Rosemary Pork with Apricot Glaze	133
Creamy Coconut Sauce on Jamaican Salmon	134
Turkey 'n Biscuit Bake	134
Chicken Bruschetta Bake	135
Amazingly Healthy Zucchini Bake	135
3-Cheese Meatball Bake	136
Tater Tot, Cheeseburger 'n Bacon Bake	136
Chicago-Style Deep Dish Pizza	137

1000 Days Air Fryer Meal Plan 138

Introduction

Air Fryer is known for being a revolutionary, brand new cooking appliance that has changed the culinary world forever. And after discovering the utility of air fryer, you will never be able to quit using this innovative cooking appliance. Therefore, if you want to start enjoying one of the best hot frying, this cookbook is the right choice for you. This book will inspire you with its wide variety of meal plan recipes and low-fat air fried dishes that are tested by professional cooks.

Through this book, you will learn all the information together with the tips that will allow you to use this cooking appliance properly. Besides, this versatile cooking appliance, Air Fryer, will display a wide range of delicious recipes from breakfast, vegetable, poultry, red meat, seafood, skewer, snack, baked.

So what are you waiting for to download this Air Fryer cookbook? This Air Fryer cookbook goes far beyond the traditional concept of frying and offers you useful tips to help you learn the major basics of using air fryers in a short time. For the first time in your life, you will learn how to make fried recipes with the same delicious fried taste, but without feeling any guilt.

Chapter 1 Go to Air Fryer

Who among us doesn't want to eat healthy food without having to give up the delicious flavour, the texture and the beautiful presentation of our favorite dishes we make every day? But what can you do if you cannot enjoy the taste of some of the most sumptuous, popular recipes that you have ever tried like onion rings, spring rolls and French fries? If you may not give up on fried foods, you can use a revolutionary cooking appliance to make it healthier. If you are wondering what this cooking appliance that can help you enjoy fried food in a healthier way is, then it is high time you purchased an Air Fryer.

Using an Air Fryer will enable you to reduce the level of saturated fat without the need to use unsaturated oils like canola oil, corn oil, peanut oil and sunflower oil. Only Air Frying food will help you lower the various health problems fried food can cause. And because all people are racing to make their cooking experience healthier, the number of purchases of Air fryers all over the world reached an unprecedented level.

Not only an Air fryer will help you bake, but it can also help you grill, roast and fry with a very little quantity of oil or with no oil at all. But have you ever wondered what an Air Fryer is? Who invented this revolutionary appliance? How does it work and most importantly, what are the main health benefits of using an Air Fryer? If you have seen hundreds of advertisements encouraging you to purchase an Air Fryer and you don't know why you should purchase your own Air Fryer, then worry no more because you have come to the right place to find all the information you need about air frying.

And just like its name suggests, Air frying is based on hot air to fry food and to cook any type of ingredients through the process of the circulation of hot air in this cooking appliance. In addition to a short introduction and a quick glimpse at the history of air frying, this air fryer cook book displays a wide range of sumptuous recipes that will make you a master chef in your own kitchen.

Air Fryer Benefits

Using Air Fryers has a variety of benefits, especially if you are always busy and on the go. Not only air fryers are useful for people seeking healthy food, but it is also of a great use to keep your food from burning.

Each Air Fryer is equipped with a system that controls the cooling system that helps protect your food from burning. Not only an air fryer can help you cook tastier food, but it will also help you cook friendly to your environment.

1. Using an Air Fryer saves about 80% of oil compared to conventional fryers
2. Air frying food lowers the level of processed fat to offer you a healthy alternative for deep fried food.
3. Cleaning an air fryer is very simple, mainly because the parts of the air fryer are easy to remove
4. Cooking with an air fryer is fast compared to other conventional frying methods. You don't need more than 15 to 20 minutes to fry your ingredients.
5. Food in your air fryer is evenly cooked because the air evenly heated equally in this cooking appliance.

Useful Tips

1. Always keep your Air Fryer out of children's reach
2. Make sure that all cords are away and safe from hot surfaces.
3. Do never connect your Air Fryer to an external timer.
4. Make sure to place your Air Fryer away from any combustible materials like curtains or tablecloths
5. Always wait 30 minutes before cleaning your Air Fryer after each use.
6. Make sure to check that the voltage is properly fits the voltage you have at home.
7. Do never seek the helped of an inexperienced person to fix any damage in the main cord or to fix your air fryer.
8. If you doubt the existence of any possible damage to the Air Fryer, plug; then make sure not to use it.
9. Do never put anything over your air fryer
10. Only use air fryers for air frying and not any other purpose

Safeguards

When using an Air Fryer, there are some important safeguards you should pay attention to for your safety and for the safety of people around you. And here are some of the most important safeguards you should know before your first use:

1. Always make sure your hands are away from the steam outlets of the air fryer
2. During hot air frying, hot steam is released through the air outlets.
3. Immediately unplug the appliance if you see dark smoke coming out of
4. Do not put air fryer under water or rinse any electrical elements.
5. Place all your ingredients in the steamer basket in order to prevent any contact from the heating components
6. Never overcrowd or fill your Air Fryer because it can damage the air fryer.

7. Be cautious when removing the steam or the water from your air fryer while it still has heat.
8. You can use a silicone oven-safe dish or a glass when making quiches, cakes and cupcakes.
9. You can also use your Air Fryer to reheat your meals at a temperature of about 300°F for about 10 minutes
10. Keep all ingredients in the basket to prevent contact from heating
11. Don't touch your air fryer from the inside while it is still under use.
12. You can add a very small quantity of oil to your air fryer to assure a crispier taste

Air Fryer Cooking Charts

Air Fryer Cooking Temperature		
INGREDIENT	TEMPERATURE	TIME
Frozen fries	390°F	20 minutes
Fresh fries	360° F	15 minutes
Chicken nuggets	390°F	15 minutes
Chicken fillet	390° F	40 minutes
Drumsticks	360° F	20 minutes
Steaks	360°F	25 minutes
Pork chops	360° F	25 minutes
Hamburger	360° F	20 minutes
Frozen fish sticks	390° F	15 minutes
Fish	325° F	15 minutes
Cup cakes and short cakes	390° F	15 minutes

1000 Days Meal Plan for Air Fryer

This cookbook offers you 1000 days meal plans that will accompany you into an enjoyable cooking journey. Besides, this book will teach you how to fry healthier food and eat healthier meals thanks to an Air Fryer. You will be surprised how unbelievable the results of air frying will be and how satisfying this cooking method is. What are you waiting for to download your own copy of this meal plan air fryer cookbook?

Keep in mind that you can't judge the use of an air fryer until you try it yourself.

We hope, from the bottom of our heart that you will benefit from this cookbook just like many other people all over the world do.

We hope that the meal plans you will find in this book will inspire you to cook balanced food for you, your family as well as your friends. Wait no more and surprise your dear family with a collection of some of the most delicious meal plans you can ever try. Whether you are a beginner or a professional, this cook book is your best choice.

Chapter 2 Air Fryer Recipes

Breakfast Recipes

Creamy Broccoli Egg Scramble

(Servings: 2, Cooking Time: 20 minutes)

Ingredients:
- 3 Eggs
- 1/2 cup Broccoli small florets
- 1/2 cup Bell Pepper cut into small pieces
- 2 tbsp Cream
- 2 tbsp Parmesan Cheese grated or cheddar cheese
- Salt to taste
- Black Pepper to taste

Directions for Cooking:
1) Lightly grease baking pan of air fryer with cooking spray. Spread broccoli florets and bell pepper on bottom and for 7 minutes, cook on 360°F.
2) Meanwhile, in a bowl whisk eggs. Stir in cream. Season with pepper and salt.
3) Remove basket and toss the mixture a bit. Pour egg mixture over.
4) Cook for another 10 minutes.
5) Sprinkle cheese and let it rest for 3 minutes.
6) Serve and enjoy.

Nutrition Information:
Calories: 273; Carbs: 5.6g; Protein: 16.1g; Fat: 20.6g

Loaded Breakfast Hash Browns

(Servings: 4, Cooking Time: 20 minutes)

Ingredients:
- 3 russet potatoes, peeled and grated
- 1/4 cup chopped green peppers
- 1/4 cup chopped red peppers
- 1/4 cup chopped onions
- 2 garlic cloves chopped
- 1 teaspoon paprika
- salt and pepper to taste
- 1 teaspoon canola oil
- 1 teaspoon olive oil

Directions for Cooking:
1) For 20 minutes, soak the grated potatoes in a bowl of cold water to make it crunchy and remove the starch. Then drain well and completely dry with paper towels.
2) Lightly grease baking pan of air fryer with cooking spray.
3) Add grated potatoes in air fryer. Season with garlic, paprika, salt, and pepper. Add canola and olive oil. Toss well to coat.
4) For 10 minutes, cook on 390ºF.
5) Remove basket and toss the mixture a bit. Stir in green and red peppers, and onions.
6) Cook for another 10 minutes.
7) Serve and enjoy.

Nutrition Information:
Calories: 263; Carbs: 53.2g; Protein: 6.5g; Fat: 2.6g

Breakfast Biscuits, Eggs 'n Bacon

(Servings: 4, Cooking Time: 28 minutes)

Ingredients:
- 5 eggs
- ¼ cup milk
- ½ of 16-ounces refrigerated breakfast biscuits
- 4 scallions, chopped
- 1 cup shredded extra sharp cheddar cheese
- 8 slices cooked center cut bacon

Directions for Cooking:
1) In baking pan cook bacon for 8 minutes at 360ºF or until crisped. Remove bacon and discard excess fat.
2) Evenly spread biscuits on bottom. For 5 minutes, cook at same temperature.
3) Meanwhile, whisk eggs, milk, and scallions.
4) Remove basket, evenly layer bacon on top of biscuit, sprinkle cheese on top, and pour eggs.
5) Cook for another 15 minutes or until eggs are set.
6) Serve and enjoy.

Nutrition Information:
Calories: 241; Carbs: 4.3g; Protein: 22.6g; Fat: 23.7g

Hash Brown, Sausage 'n Cauliflower Bake

(Servings: 3, Cooking Time: 27 minutes)

Ingredients:
- 1-pound hot pork sausage, diced
- 1/2 (30 ounce) package frozen hash brown potatoes, thawed
- ½ cup shredded Cheddar cheese
- 1 teaspoons salt
- 1/2 teaspoon ground black pepper
- ½ cup milk
- 1 small cauliflower, riced
- 3 large eggs

Directions for Cooking:
1) Lightly grease baking pan of air fryer with cooking spray. And add diced sausage and cook for 10 minutes on 360°F.
2) Add hash brown and riced cauliflower. Cook for another 5 minutes.
3) Meanwhile, whisk well eggs, salt, pepper, and milk.
4) Remove basket and toss the mixture a bit. Evenly spread cheese and pour eggs.
5) Cook for another 12 minutes or until set
6) Serve and enjoy.

Nutrition Information:
Calories: 612; Carbs: 33.4g; Protein: 49.2g; Fat: 44.6g

Cauliflower-Broccoli Egg Bake

(Servings: 3, Cooking Time: 20 minutes)

Ingredients:
- 1/2-pound hot pork sausage, diced
- ½ cup shredded Cheddar cheese
- 1 teaspoons salt
- 1/2 teaspoon ground black pepper
- ½ cup milk
- 1 cup cauliflower, riced
- 1 cup broccoli, cut into little bits or riced
- 3 large eggs

Directions for Cooking:
1) Lightly grease baking pan of air fryer with cooking spray. And cook pork sausage for 5 minutes at 360°F.
2) Remove basket and toss the mixture a bit. Stir in riced cauliflower and broccoli. Cook for another 5 minutes.
3) Meanwhile, whisk well eggs, salt, pepper, and milk. Stir in cheese.
4) Remove basket and pour in egg mixture.
5) Cook for another 10 minutes.
6) Serve and enjoy.

Nutrition Information:
Calories: 434; Carbs: 6.5g; Protein: 27.3g; Fat: 33.2g

Raisin 'n Apple French Toast

(Servings: 6, Cooking Time: 40 minutes)

Ingredients:
- ½-lb loaf cinnamon raisin bread, cubed
- 4-oz cream cheese, diced
- ½ cup diced peeled apples
- 4 eggs
- 1 ¼ cups half-and-half cream
- 3 tbsp butter, melted
- 2 tbsp maple syrup

Directions for Cooking:
1) Lightly grease baking pan of air fryer with cooking spray.
2) Evenly spread half of the bread on bottom of pan. Sprinkle evenly the cream cheese and apples. Add remaining bread on top.
3) In a large bowl, whisk well eggs, cream, butter, and maple syrup. Pour over bread mixture.
4) Cover air fryer baking pan with plastic wrap and refrigerate for two hours.
5) Preheat air fryer to 325°F.
6) Cook for 40 minutes.
7) Serve and enjoy while warm.

Nutrition Information:
Calories: 362; Carbs: 28.3g; Protein: 10.1g; Fat: 23.1g

Overnight French Toast with Blueberries

(Servings: 5, Cooking Time: 45 minutes)

Ingredients:
- 6 slices day-old bread, cut into 1-inch cubes
- 1 (8 ounce) package cream cheese, cut into 1-inch cubes
- 1 cup fresh blueberries, divided
- 6 eggs, beaten
- 1 cup milk
- 1/2 teaspoon vanilla extract
- 2 tablespoons and 2 teaspoons maple syrup
- 1/2 cup white sugar
- 1 tablespoon cornstarch
- 1/2 cup water
- 1-1/2 teaspoons butter

Directions for Cooking:
1) Lightly grease baking pan of air fryer with cooking spray.
2) Evenly spread half of the bread on bottom of pan. Sprinkle evenly the cream cheese and ½ cup blueberries. Add remaining bread on top.
3) In a large bowl, whisk well eggs, milk, syrup, and vanilla extract. Pour over bread mixture.
4) Cover air fryer baking pan with foil and refrigerate overnight.
5) Preheat air fryer to 330°F.
6) Cook for 25 minutes covered in foil, remove foil and cook for another 20 minutes or until middle is set.
7) Meanwhile, make the sauce by mixing cornstarch, water, and sugar in a saucepan and bring to a boil. Stir in remaining blueberries and simmer until thickened and blueberries have burst.
8) Serve and enjoy with blueberry syrup.

Nutrition Information:
Calories: 492; Carbs: 51.9g; Protein: 15.1g; Fat: 24.8g

Eggs Benedict in an Overnight Casserole

(Servings: 5, Cooking Time: 40 minutes)

Ingredients:
- 4 large eggs
- 1 cup milk
- 1 stalk green onions, chopped
- ½ tsp onion powder
- 1/2 teaspoon salt
- 6-ounces Canadian bacon, cut into 1/2-inch dice
- 3 English muffins, cut into 1/2-inch dice
- 1/4 teaspoon paprika
- 1/2 (.9 ounce) package hollandaise sauce mix
- 1/2 cup milk
- 2 tablespoons margarine

Directions for Cooking:
1) Lightly grease baking pan of air fryer with cooking spray.
2) Place half of the bacon on bottom of pan, evenly spread died English muffins on top. Evenly spread remaining bacon on top.
3) In a large bowl, whisk well eggs, 1 cup milk, green onions, onion powder, and salt. Pour over English muffin mixture. Sprinkle top with paprika. Cover with foil and refrigerate overnight.
4) Preheat air fryer to 390°F.
5) Cook in air fryer covered in foil for 25 minutes. Remove foil and continue cooking for another 15 minutes or until set.
6) Meanwhile, make the hollandaise sauce by melting margarine in a sauce pan. Mix remaining milk and hollandaise sauce in a small bowl and whisk into melted margarine. Simmer until thickened while continuously stirring.
7) Serve and enjoy with sauce.

Nutrition Information:
Calories: 282; Carbs: 21.2g; Protein: 17.5g; Fat: 14.1g

Egg-Substitute 'n Bacon Casserole

(Servings: 4. Cooking Time: 35 minutes)

Ingredients:
- 4 frozen hash brown patties
- 1 (6 ounce) package Canadian bacon, quartered
- 2 cups shredded Cheddar-Monterey Jack cheese blend
- 3/4 cup and 2 tablespoons egg substitute (such as Egg Beaters® Southwestern Style)
- 1/2 cup 2% milk
- 1/4 teaspoon salt
- 1/4 teaspoon ground mustard

Directions for Cooking:
1) Lightly grease baking pan of air fryer with cooking spray.
2) Evenly spread hash brown patties on bottom of pan. Top evenly with bacon and then followed by cheese.
3) In a bowl, whisk well mustard, salt, milk, and egg substitute. Pour over bacon mixture.
4) Cover air fryer baking pan with foil.
5) Preheat air fryer to 330°F.
6) Cook for another 20 minutes, remove foil and continue cooking for another 15 minutes or until eggs are set.
7) Serve and enjoy.

Nutrition Information:
Calories: 459; Carbs: 21.0g; Protein: 29.4g; Fat: 28.5g

Country style Brekky Casserole

(Servings: 4, Cooking Time: 45 minutes)

Ingredients:
- 8-ounce bulk breakfast sausage
- 1 stalk green onion, chopped
- 8-ounce package hash brown potatoes
- 1 cup shredded Cheddar cheese
- 3 eggs, lightly beaten
- 1/2 cup milk
- 1/2 (2.64-ounce) package country gravy mix
- A dash of paprika or to taste (optional)

Directions for Cooking:
1) Lightly grease baking pan of air fryer with cooking spray.
2) For 10 minutes, cook sausage and crumble at 360°F. Halfway through cooking time, open air fryer and continue crumbling sausage.
3) Once done cooking remove excess oil.
4) Stir in green onions and evenly spread crumbled sausage. Spread hash brown on top and sprinkle evenly with cheese.
5) In a bowl, whisk well gravy, milk, and eggs until smooth. Pour over cheese mixture. Sprinkle top with paprika.
6) Cover pan with foil.
7) Cook for 20 minutes, remove foil and cook for another 10 minutes.
8) Let it stand for 5 minutes.
9) Serve and enjoy.

Nutrition Information:
Calories: 406; Carbs: 13.3g; Protein: 21.7g; Fat: 29.5g

Amish Style Brekky Casserole

(Servings: 6, Cooking Time: 45 minutes)

Ingredients:
- 1/2-pound sliced bacon, diced
- 1/2 sweet onion, chopped
- 2 cups frozen shredded hash brown potatoes, thawed
- 5 medium eggs, lightly beaten
- 1 cup shredded Cheddar cheese
- 3/4 cup small curd cottage cheese
- 1/2 cup and 2 tablespoons shredded Swiss cheese

Directions for Cooking:
1) Lightly grease baking pan of air fryer with cooking spray.
2) For 10 minutes, cook on 330°F the onion and bacon. Discard excess fat.
3) Meanwhile, in a bowl, whisk well Swiss cheese, cottage cheese, cheddar cheese, eggs, and potatoes. Pour into pan of cooked bacon and mix well.
4) Cook for another 25 minutes.
5) Let it stand in air fryer for another 10 minutes.
6) Serve and enjoy.

Nutrition Information:
Calories: 341; Carbs: 12.1g; Protein: 21.7g; Fat: 22.8g

Baked Cornbread and Eggs

(Servings: 3, Cooking Time: 45 minutes)

Ingredients:
- 1/2 cup chopped onion
- 1 stalk celery, diced
- 2 cups diced cooked ham
- 1/2 (14.5 ounce) can chicken broth
- 1/4 cup water
- 1/4 cup butter
- 1/2 (14-ounce) package seasoned cornbread stuffing mix
- 3 eggs
- 3/4 cup shredded Cheddar cheese
- 1/4 teaspoon paprika, for garnish

Directions for Cooking:
1) Lightly grease baking pan of air fryer with cooking spray. Add celery and onions.
2) For 5 minutes, cook on 360ºF. Open and stir in ham. Cook for another 5 minutes.
3) Open and stir in butter, water, and chicken broth. Mix well and continue cooking for another 5 minutes.
4) Toss in stuffing mix and toss well to coat. Cover pan with foil.
5) Cook for another 15 minutes.
6) Remove foil and make 3 indentation in the stuffing to hold an egg. Break an egg in each hole.
7) Cook uncovered for another 10 minutes or until egg is cooked to desired doneness.
8) Sprinkle with cheese and paprika. Let it stand in air fryer for another 5 minutes.
9) Serve and enjoy.

Nutrition Information:
Calories: 847; Carbs: 54.4g; Protein: 37.5g; Fat: 53.2g

Feta and Spinach Brekky Pie

(Servings: 3, Cooking Time: 30 minutes)

Ingredients:
- 1 1/2 teaspoons butter
- 1/2-pound fresh spinach
- 6 eggs
- salt and freshly ground black pepper to taste
- 1/2 pinch cayenne pepper
- 3 slices bacon, chopped
- 1/4 onion, diced
- 1/2 pinch salt
- 1-1/2 ounces crumbled feta cheese

Directions for Cooking:
1) Lightly grease baking pan of air fryer with butter. Add spinach and for 2 minutes, cook on 360ºF.
2) Drain well the spinach and squeeze dry. Chop and set aside.
3) Add bacon in air fryer pan and cook for 6 minutes or until crisped. Discard excess fat.
4) Stir in onion and season with salt. Cook for another 5 minutes. Stir in chopped spinach and cook for another 5 minutes to heat through.
5) Meanwhile, in a bowl whisk well eggs, cayenne pepper, black pepper, and salt.
6) Remove basket, evenly spread mixture in pan, and pour in eggs. Sprinkle feta cheese on top.
7) Cook for another 15 minutes, until eggs are cooked to desired doneness.
8) Serve and enjoy.

Nutrition Information:
Calories: 273; Carbs: 5.1g; Protein: 20.3g; Fat: 19.0g

Cheesy-Bacon Casserole

(Servings: 6, Cooking Time: 50 minutes)

Ingredients:
- 4 slices bread, crusts removed
- 1 1/2 cups skim milk
- 1 cup egg substitute (such as Egg Beaters®)
- 1 tablespoon chopped fresh chives
- 6 slices cooked bacon, crumbled
- 1 cup Cheddar cheese

Directions for Cooking:
1) Cook bacon in baking pan of air fryer for 10 minutes at 360°F. Once done, discard excess fat and then crumble bacon.
2) In a bowl, whisk well eggs. Stir in milk and chives.
3) In same air fryer baking pan, evenly spread bread slices. Pour egg mixture over it. Top with bacon. Cover pan with foil and let it rest in the fridge for at least an hour.
4) Preheat air fryer to 330°F.
5) Cook while covered in foil for 20 minutes. Remove foil and sprinkle cheese. Continue cooking uncovered for another 15 minutes.
6) Serve and enjoy.

Nutrition Information:
Calories: 207; Carbs: 12.1g; Protein: 15.3g; Fat: 10.8g

Mixed Vegetable Frittata

(Servings: 6, Cooking Time: 45 minutes)

Ingredients:
- 8-ounces frozen mixed vegetables (bell peppers, broccoli, etc.), thawed
- ½-pound breakfast sausage
- 1 cup cheddar cheese shredded
- 6 eggs
- 1/2 cup milk or cream
- 1 teaspoon kosher salt
- 1/2 teaspoon black pepper

Directions for Cooking:
1) Lightly grease baking pan of air fryer with cooking spray. For 10 minutes, cook on 360°F the breakfast sausage and crumble. Halfway through cooking time, crumble sausage some more until it looks like ground meat. Once done cooking, discard excess fat.
2) Stir in thawed mixed vegetables and cook for 7 minutes or until heated through, stirring halfway through cooking time.
3) Meanwhile, in a bowl, whisk well eggs, cream, salt, and pepper.
4) Remove basket, evenly spread vegetable mixture, and pour in egg mixture. Cover pan with foil.
5) Cook for another 15 minutes, remove foil and continue cooking for another 5-10 minutes or until eggs are set to desired doneness.
6) Serve and enjoy.

Nutrition Information:
Calories: 187; Carbs: 7.0g; Protein: 15.0g; Fat: 11.0g

Breakfast Chicken Casserole

(Servings: 2, Cooking Time: 35 minutes)

Ingredients:
- 1-1/4 cups cooked chopped broccoli
- 1 cup shredded, cooked chicken meat
- 1 (4.5 ounce) can mushrooms, drained
- 1/2 (8 ounce) can water chestnuts, drained (optional)
- 1 (10.75 ounce) can condensed cream of chicken soup
- 1/2 cup mayonnaise
- 1/2 teaspoon lemon juice
- 1/8 teaspoon curry powder
- 1 1/2 teaspoons melted butter
- 1/4 cup shredded Cheddar cheese

Directions for Cooking:
1) Lightly grease baking pan of air fryer with cooking spray.
2) Evenly spread broccoli on bottom of pan. Sprinkle chicken on top, followed by water chestnuts and mushrooms.
3) In a bowl, whisk well melted butter, curry powder, lemon juice, mayonnaise, and soup. Pour over chicken mixture in pan. Cover pan with foil.
4) For 25 minutes, cook on 360°F.
5) Remove foil from pan and cook for another 10 minutes or until top is a golden brown.
6) Serve and enjoy.

Nutrition Information:
Calories: 532; Carbs: 18.0g; Protein: 20.0g; Fat: 42.2g

Rice Casserole Mexican Style

(Servings: 4, Cooking Time: 50 minutes)

Ingredients:
- 1-1/3 cups water
- 2/3 cup uncooked long grain white rice
- 1/2-pound ground pork breakfast sausage
- 8-ounce picante sauce
- 4-ounce sour cream
- 1/4-pound Cheddar cheese, shredded

Directions for Cooking:
1) Lightly grease baking pan of air fryer with cooking spray. For 10 minutes, cook on 360°F the sausage. Crumble sausage halfway through cooking time.
2) Meanwhile, add water in a saucepan and bring to a boil. Once boiling, stir in rice. Cover and cook on low fire for 20 minutes.
3) Once sausage is done cooking, discard excess fat. Stir in sour cream and picante sauce. Mix well.
4) Once rice is done cooking, fluff rice and mix into sour cream mixture. Toss well to coat. Sprinkle cheese on top. Cover pan with foil.
5) Cook for 15 minutes, remove foil and cook for another 5 minutes.
6) Serve and enjoy.

Nutrition Information:
Calories: 452; Carbs: 31.0g; Protein: 18.9g; Fat: 28.0g

Broccoli, Ham 'n Potato Casserole

(Servings: 3, Cooking Time: 35 minutes)

Ingredients:
- 6-ounce frozen French fries
- 6-ounce frozen chopped broccoli
- 3/4 cup 3/cooked, cubed ham
- 1/3 cup canned condensed cream of mushroom soup
- 1/3 cup milk
- 1 1/2 tablespoon mayonnaise
- 1/3 cup grated Parmesan cheese

Directions for Cooking:
1) Lightly grease baking pan of air fryer with cooking spray.
2) Evenly spread French fries on bottom of pan. Place broccoli on top in a single layer. Evenly spread ham.
3) In a bowl, whisk well mayonnaise, milk, and soup. Pour over fries mixture.
4) Sprinkle cheese and over pan with foil.
5) For 25 minutes, cook on 390°F. Remove foil and continue cooking for another 10 minutes.
6) Serve and enjoy.

Nutrition Information:
Calories: 511; Carbs: 34.7g; Protein: 22.8g; Fat: 31.2g

Cheeseburger and Bacon Casserole

(Servings: 4, Cooking Time: 40 minutes)

Ingredients:
- 1 cup ground beef
- 1 clove garlic, minced
- 1/8 teaspoon onion powder
- 4 slices of bacon, cut into small pieces
- 3 eggs
- 1/3 cup heavy whipping cream
- 1/8 teaspoon salt
- 1/8 teaspoon ground black pepper
- 4.5-ounce shredded Cheddar cheese, divided

Directions for Cooking:
1) Lightly grease baking pan of air fryer with cooking spray. Add ground beef, garlic, and onion powder. For 10 minutes, cook on 360°F. Stirring halfway through cooking time.
2) Drain excess fat.
3) Evenly spread ground beef. Place bacon slices on top.
4) In a bowl, whisk well pepper, salt, cream, and eggs. Pour over bacon. Sprinkle cheese on top.
5) Cover pan with foil.
6) Cook for 20 minutes, remove foil and continue cooking for another 10 minutes.
7) Serve and enjoy.

Nutrition Information:
Calories: 454; Carbs: 1.6g; Protein: 28.7g; Fat: 36.9g

Main Meal Recipes

Turkey 'n Broccoli Bake

(Servings: 4, Cooking Time: 40 minutes)

Ingredients:
- 1/2 cup uncooked white rice
- 1 cup cooked, chopped turkey meat
- 1/2 (10 ounce) package frozen broccoli, thawed
- 1/2 cup shredded Cheddar cheese
- 1/2 (7 ounce) package whole wheat crackers, crushed
- 1 tablespoon and 1-1/2 teaspoons butter, melted

Directions for Cooking:
1) Bring to a boil 2 cups of water in a saucepan. Stir in rice and simmer for 20 minutes. Turn off fire and set aside.
2) Lightly grease baking pan of air fryer with cooking spray. Mix in cooked rice, cheese, broccoli, and turkey. Toss well to mix.
3) Mix well melted butter and crushed crackers in a small bowl. Evenly spread on top of rice.
4) For 20 minutes, cook on 360°F until tops are lightly browned.
5) Serve and enjoy.

Nutrition Information:
Calories: 269; Carbs: 23.7g; Protein: 17.0g; Fat: 11.8g

Penne Chicken Pesto Bake

(Servings: 3, Cooking Time: 25 minutes)

Ingredients:
- 2 tablespoons seasoned bread crumbs
- 2 tablespoons grated Parmesan cheese
- 3/4 teaspoon olive oil
- 4-ounce penne pasta, cooked according to manufacturer's Directions for Cooking:
- 1-1/2 cups cubed cooked chicken
- 1 cup shredded Italian cheese blend
- 3/4 cup fresh baby spinach
- 1/4 (15 ounce) can crushed tomatoes
- 1/4 (15 ounce) jar Alfredo sauce
- 1/4 (15 ounce) jar pesto sauce
- 1/3 cup milk

Directions for Cooking:

1) In a small bowl, whisk well olive oil, Parmesan, and bread crumbs. Set aside.
2) Lightly grease baking pan of air fryer with cooking spray. Mix in milk, pesto sauce, alfredo sauce, tomatoes, spinach, and Italian cheese blend. Mix well. Toss in cooked pasta and toss well to coat. Evenly sprinkle bread crumb mixture on top.
3) For 25 minutes, cook on 360°F until tops are lightly browned.
4) Serve and enjoy.

Nutrition Information:
Calories: 729; Carbs: 40.7g; Protein: 45.4g; Fat: 47.2g

Green Bean Chicken Stuffing Bake

(Servings: 3, Cooking Time: 20 minutes)

Ingredients:
- 1 cup cooked, cubed chicken breast meat
- 1/2 (10.75 ounce) can condensed cream of chicken soup
- 1/2 (14.5 ounce) can green beans, drained
- salt and pepper to taste
- 6-ounce unseasoned dry bread stuffing mix
- 1/2 cup shredded Cheddar cheese

Directions for Cooking:
1) Mix well pepper, salt, soup, and chicken in a medium bowl.
2) Make the stuffing according to package Directions for Cooking.
3) Lightly grease baking pan of air fryer with cooking spray. Evenly spread chicken mixture on bottom of pan. Top evenly with stuffing. Sprinkle cheese on top.
4) Cover pan with foil.
5) For 15 minutes, cook on 390°F.
6) Remove foil and cook for 5 minutes at 390°F until tops are lightly browned.
7) Serve and enjoy.

Nutrition Information:
Calories: 418; Carbs: 48.8g; Protein: 27.1g; Fat: 12.7g

Cheesy Broccoli-Rice Bake

(Servings: 4, Cooking Time: 28 minutes)

Ingredients:
- 1 cup water
- 1 cup uncooked instant rice
- 1 (10 ounce) can chunk chicken, drained
- 1/2 (10.75 ounce) can condensed cream of mushroom soup
- 1/2 (10.75 ounce) can condensed cream of chicken soup
- 2 tablespoons butter
- 1/2 cup milk
- 8-ounce frozen chopped broccoli
- 1/2 small white onion, chopped
- 1/2-pound processed cheese food

Directions for Cooking:

1) Lightly grease baking pan of air fryer with cooking spray. Add water and bring to a boil at 390°F. Stir in rice and cook for 3 minutes.
2) Stir in processed cheese, onion, broccoli, milk, butter, chicken soup, mushroom soup, and chicken. Mix well.
3) Cook for 15 minutes at 390°F, fluff mixture and continue cooking for another 10 minutes until tops are browned.
4) Serve and enjoy.

Nutrition Information:
Calories: 752; Carbs: 82.7g; Protein: 36.0g; Fat: 30.8g

Rice Casserole Mexican Style

(Servings: 4, Cooking Time: 45 minutes)

Ingredients:
- 1-1/3 cups water
- 2/3 cup uncooked long grain white rice
- 1/2-pound ground pork breakfast sausage
- 1/2 (16 ounce) jar picante sauce
- 1/2 (8 ounce) container sour cream
- 1/4-pound Cheddar cheese, shredded

Directions for Cooking:
1) Ring water to a boil in a saucepan and stir in rice. Cover and simmer for 20 minutes until all liquid is absorbed. Turn off fire and fluff rice.
2) Lightly grease baking pan of air fryer with cooking spray. Add sausage and cook for 10 minutes at 360°F. Halfway through cooking time, crumble and stir sausage.
3) Stir in cooked rice, sour cream, and picante sauce. Mix well. Sprinkle cheese on top
4) Cook for 15 minutes at 390°F until tops are lightly browned.
5) Serve and enjoy.

Nutrition Information:
Calories: 452; Carbs: 31.0g; Protein: 18.9g; Fat: 28.0g

Mouth-Watering Taco Bake

(Servings: 5, Cooking Time: 25 minutes)

Ingredients:
- 1/2-pound lean ground beef
- 1/4-pound macaroni, cooked according to manufacturer's Directions for Cooking:
- 1/4 cup chopped onion
- 1/2 (10.75 ounce) can condensed tomato soup
- 1/2 (14.5 ounce) can diced tomatoes
- 1/2 (1.25 ounce) package taco seasoning mix
- 1-ounce shredded Cheddar cheese
- 1-ounce shredded Monterey Jack cheese
- 1/2 cup crushed tortilla chips
- 1/4 cup sour cream (optional)
- 2 tablespoons chopped green onions

Directions for Cooking:
1) Lightly grease baking pan of air fryer with cooking spray. Add onion and ground beef. For 10 minutes, cook on 360°F. Halfway through cooking time, stir and crumble ground beef.
2) Add taco seasoning, diced tomatoes, and tomato soup. Mix well. Mix in pasta.
3) Sprinkle crushed tortilla chips. Sprinkle cheese.
4) Cook for 15 minutes at 390°F until tops are lightly browned and cheese is melted.
5) Serve and enjoy.

Nutrition Information:
Calories: 329; Carbs: 28.2g; Protein: 15.6g; Fat: 17.0g

A Different Rice-Chik'n Bake

(Servings: 3, Cooking Time: 45 minutes)

Ingredients:
- 3 chicken breasts, cut into cubes
- 2 cups water
- 2 cups instant white rice
- 1 (10.75 ounce) can cream of chicken soup
- 1 (10.75 ounce) can cream of celery soup
- 1 (10.75 ounce) can cream of mushroom soup
- salt and ground black pepper to taste
- 1/2 cup butter, sliced into pats

Directions for Cooking:
1) Lightly grease baking pan of air fryer with cooking spray.
2) In pan, mix cream of mushroom, celery soup, chicken soup, rice, water and chicken. Mix well.
3) Season with pepper and salt. Top with butter pats.
4) Cover pan with foil and for 35 minutes, cook on 360°F.
5) Let it stand for 10 minutes.
6) Serve and enjoy.

Nutrition Information:
Calories: 439; Carbs: 36.7g; Protein: 16.8g; Fat: 25.0g

Chicken Florentine Bake

(Servings: 2, Cooking Time: 40 minutes)

Ingredients:
- 2 skinless, boneless chicken breast halves
- 2 tablespoons butter
- 1-1/2 teaspoons minced garlic
- 1-1/2 teaspoons lemon juice
- 1/2 (10.75 ounce) can condensed cream of mushroom soup
- 1-1/2 teaspoons Italian seasoning
- 1/4 cup half-and-half
- 1/4 cup grated Parmesan cheese
- 1 (13.5 ounce) can spinach, drained
- 2 ounces fresh mushrooms, sliced
- 1/3 cup bacon bits
- 1 cup shredded mozzarella cheese

Directions for Cooking:
1) Lightly grease baking pan of air fryer with cooking spray. Add chicken breast and for 20 minutes, cook on 360°F. Halfway through cooking time, turnover chicken breast. Once done, transfer to a plate and set aside.
2) In same baking pan, melt butter. Stir in Parmesan cheese, half and half, Italian seasoning, mushroom soup, lemon juice, and garlic. Mix well and cook for 5 minutes or until heated through.
3) Stir in spinach and chicken. Tope with bacon bits and mozzarella cheese.
4) Cook for 15 minutes at 390°F until tops are lightly browned.
5) Serve and enjoy.

Nutrition Information:
Calories: 659; Carbs: 17.6g; Protein: 61.6g; Fat: 38.0g

Sea Scallop Bake

(Servings: 4, Cooking Time: 10 minutes)

Ingredients:
- 16 sea scallops, rinsed and drained
- 5 tablespoons butter, melted
- 5 cloves garlic, minced
- 2 shallots, chopped
- 3 pinches ground nutmeg
- salt and pepper to taste
- 1 cup bread crumbs
- 4 tablespoons olive oil
- 1/4 cup chopped parsley

Directions for Cooking:
1) Lightly grease baking pan of air fryer with cooking spray.
2) Mix in shallots, garlic, melted butter, and scallops. Season with pepper, salt, and nutmeg.
3) In a small bowl, whisk well olive oil and bread crumbs. Sprinkle over scallops.
4) For 10 minutes, cook on 390°F until tops are lightly browned.
5) Serve and enjoy with a sprinkle of parsley.

Nutrition Information:
Calories: 452; Carbs: 29.8g; Protein: 15.2g; Fat: 30.2g

Shrimp Casserole Louisiana Style

(Servings: 2, Cooking Time: 35 minutes)

Ingredients:
- 3/4 cup uncooked instant rice
- 3/4 cup water
- 1/2 teaspoon vegetable oil
- 1/2-pound small shrimp, peeled and deveined
- 1 tablespoon butter
- 1/2 (4 ounce) can sliced mushrooms, drained
- 1/2 (10.75 ounce) can condensed cream of shrimp soup
- 1/2 (8 ounce) container sour cream
- 1/3 cup shredded Cheddar cheese

Directions for Cooking:

1) Lightly grease baking pan of air fryer with cooking spray. Add rice, water, mushrooms, and butter. Cover with foil. For 20 minutes, cook on 360°F.
2) Open foil cover, stir in shrimps, return foil and let it rest for 5 minutes.
3) Remove foil completely and stir in sour cream. Mix well and evenly spread rice.
4) Top with cheese.
5) Cook for 7 minutes at 390°F until tops are lightly browned.
6) Serve and enjoy.

Nutrition Information:
Calories: 569; Carbs: 38.5g; Protein: 31.8g; Fat: 31.9g

Cheesy Zucchini-Squash Bake

(Servings: 4, Cooking Time: 30 minutes)

Ingredients:
- 1/2-pound yellow squash, sliced
- 1/2-pound zucchini, sliced
- 1/4 onion, diced
- 1/2 cup shredded Cheddar cheese
- 1/4 cup biscuit baking mix (such as Bisquick®)
- 1/4 cup butter
- 1 egg
- 1-1/2 teaspoons white sugar
- 1/2 teaspoon salt
- 5 saltine crackers, or as needed, crushed
- 2 tablespoons bread crumbs

Directions for Cooking:

1) Lightly grease baking pan of air fryer with cooking spray. Add onion, zucchini, and yellow squash. Cover pan with foil and for 15 minutes, cook on 360°F or until tender.
2) Stir in salt, sugar, egg, butter, baking mix, and cheddar cheese. Mix well. Fold in crushed crackers. Top with bread crumbs.
3) Cook for 15 minutes at 390°F until tops are lightly browned.
4) Serve and enjoy.

Nutrition Information:
Calories: 285; Carbs: 16.4g; Protein: 8.6g; Fat: 20.5g

Portuguese Bacalao Tapas

(Servings: 4, Cooking Time: 26 minutes)

Ingredients:
- 1-pound cod fish filet, chopped
- 2 Yukon Gold potatoes, peeled and diced
- 2 tablespoon butter
- 1 yellow onions, thinly sliced
- 1 clove garlic, chopped, divided
- 1/4 cup chopped fresh parsley, divided
- 1/4 cup olive oil
- 3/4 teaspoon red pepper flakes
- freshly ground pepper to taste
- 2 hard cooked eggs, chopped
- 5 pitted green olives
- 5 pitted black olives

Directions for Cooking:

1) Lightly grease baking pan of air fryer with cooking spray. Add and melt butter at 360°F. Stir in onions and cook for 6 minutes until caramelized.
2) Stir in black pepper, red pepper flakes, half of parsley, garlic, olive oil, diced potatoes and chopped fish. For 10 minutes, cook on 360°F. Halfway through cooking time, stir well to mix.
3) Cook for 10 minutes at 390°F until tops are lightly browned.
4) Garnish with remaining parsley, eggs, black and green olives.
5) Serve and enjoy with chips.

Nutrition Information:
Calories: 691; Carbs: 25.2g; Protein: 77.1g; Fat: 31.3g

Zucchini & Carrot Bake

(Servings: 4, Cooking Time: 25 minutes)

Ingredients:
- 1/2-pound carrots, sliced
- 1-1/2 zucchinis, sliced
- 1/4 cup water
- 1/4 cup mayonnaise
- 1 tablespoon grated onion
- 1/4 teaspoon prepared horseradish
- 1/4 teaspoon salt
- 1/4 teaspoon ground black pepper
- 1/4 cup Italian bread crumbs
- 2 tablespoons butter, melted

Directions for Cooking:

1) Lightly grease baking pan of air fryer with cooking spray. Add carrots. For 8 minutes, cook on 360°F. Add zucchini and continue cooking for another 5 minutes.
2) Meanwhile, in a bowl whisk well pepper, salt, horseradish, onion, mayonnaise, and water. Pour into pan of veggies. Toss well to coat.
3) In a small bowl mix melted butter and bread crumbs. Sprinkle over veggies.
4) Cook for 10 minutes at 390°F until tops are lightly browned.
5) Serve and enjoy.

Nutrition Information:
Calories: 223; Carbs: 13.8g; Protein: 2.7g; Fat: 17.4g

Cheesy-Creamy Broccoli Bake

(Servings: 2, Cooking Time: 30 minutes)

Ingredients:
- 1-pound fresh broccoli, coarsely chopped
- 1/2 large onion, coarsely chopped
- 1/4 cup water
- 2 tablespoons all-purpose flour
- 1/2 (14 ounce) can evaporated milk, divided
- salt to taste
- 1/2 cup cubed sharp Cheddar cheese
- 1 tablespoon dry bread crumbs, or to taste
- 1-1/2 teaspoons butter, or to taste

Directions for Cooking:
1) Lightly grease baking pan of air fryer with cooking spray. Mix in half of the milk and flour in pan and for 5 minutes, cook on 360°F. Halfway through cooking time, mix well. Add broccoli and remaining milk. Mix well and cook for another 5 minutes.
2) Stir in cheese and mix well until melted.
3) In a small bowl mix well, butter and bread crumbs. Sprinkle on top of broccoli.
4) Cook for 20 minutes at 360°F until tops are lightly browned.
5) Serve and enjoy.

Nutrition Information:
Calories: 444; Carbs: 37.3g; Protein: 23.1g; Fat: 22.4g

Mushroom 'n Spinach Casserole

(Servings: 3, Cooking Time: 25 minutes)

Ingredients:
- 1 tablespoon butter
- 1/2-pound fresh mushrooms, sliced
- 1 (10 ounce) package fresh spinach, rinsed and stems removed
- 1/2 teaspoon salt
- 2 tablespoons butter, melted
- 2 tablespoons finely chopped onion
- 3/4 cup shredded Cheddar cheese, divided

Directions for Cooking:
1) Lightly grease baking pan of air fryer with butter and melt for 2 minutes at 360°F. Stir in mushrooms and cook for 10 minutes. Halfway through cooking time, stir and mix around.
2) Stir in spinach and cook until wilted, around 5 minutes. Stirring halfway through cooking time.
3) Stir in remaining ingredients and give it a good mix.
4) Cook for 15 minutes at 390°F until tops are lightly browned.
5) Serve and enjoy.

Nutrition Information:
Calories: 229; Carbs: 7.5g; Protein: 11.3g; Fat: 21.5g

Potato Casserole Twice Baked

(Servings: 4, Cooking Time: 45 minutes)

Ingredients:
- 1 teaspoon vegetable oil, or as needed
- 1/2-pound unpeeled russet potatoes, scrubbed
- 1-1/2 cups sour cream
- 1 cup shredded Monterey Jack cheese
- 1 cup shredded Cheddar cheese
- 2-1/2 ounces cooked bacon, crumbled
- 2-1/2 green onions, chopped
- 1/8 teaspoon salt
- 1/8 teaspoon ground black pepper

Directions for Cooking:
1) Lightly grease baking pan of air fryer with cooking spray.
2) Pierce potatoes many times with fork and place in pan. For 30 minutes, cook on 390°F.
3) Remove potatoes and when cool enough to handle, chop into 1-inch cubes.
4) In same pan, mix in pepper, salt, green onions, bacon, cheddar cheese, Monterey Jack cheese, and sour cream. Mix well. Toss in potatoes and toss well to coat.
5) Cook for 15 minutes at 390°F until tops are lightly browned.
6) Serve and enjoy.

Nutrition Information:
Calories: 567; Carbs: 15.1g; Protein: 25.0g; Fat: 45.1g

Chili Rellenos Bake

(Servings: 3, Cooking Time: 30 minutes)

Ingredients:
- 1 (7 ounce) can whole green Chile peppers, drained
- 1/4-pound Monterey Jack cheese, shredded
- 1/4-pound Longhorn or Cheddar cheese, shredded
- 1 egg, beaten
- 1/2 (5 ounce) can evaporated milk
- 1 tablespoon all-purpose flour
- 1/4 cup milk
- 1/2 (8 ounce) can tomato sauce

Directions for Cooking:
1) Lightly grease baking pan of air fryer with cooking spray. Evenly spread chilies and sprinkle cheddar and Jack cheese on top.
2) In a bowl whisk well flour, milk, and eggs. Pour over chilies.
3) For 20 minutes, cook on 360°F.
4) Add tomato sauce on top.
5) Cook for 10 minutes at 390°F until tops are lightly browned.
6) Serve and enjoy.

Nutrition Information:
Calories: 392; Carbs: 12.0g; Protein: 23.9g; Fat: 27.6g

Spicy Zucchini Bake Mexican Style

(Servings: 4, Cooking Time: 30 minutes)

Ingredients:
- 1 tablespoon olive oil
- 1-1/2 pounds zucchini, cubed
- 1/2 cup chopped onion
- 1/2 teaspoon garlic salt
- 1/2 teaspoon paprika
- 1/2 teaspoon dried oregano
- 1/2 teaspoon cayenne pepper, or to taste
- 1/2 cup cooked long-grain rice
- 1/2 cup cooked pinto beans
- 1-1/4 cups salsa
- 3/4 cup shredded Cheddar cheese

Directions for Cooking:
1) Lightly grease baking pan of air fryer with olive oil. Add onions and zucchini and for 10 minutes, cook on 360ºF. Halfway through cooking time, stir.
2) Season with cayenne, oregano, paprika, and garlic salt. Mix well.
3) Stir in salsa, beans, and rice. Cook for 5 minutes.
4) Stir in cheddar cheese and mix well.
5) Cover pan with foil.
6) Cook for 15 minutes at 390ºF until bubbly.
7) Serve and enjoy.

Nutrition Information:
Calories: 263; Carbs: 24.6g; Protein: 12.5g; Fat: 12.7g

Feta-Spinach 'n Pita Casserole

(Servings: 3, Cooking Time: 5 minutes)

Ingredients:
- 3-ounce sun-dried tomato pesto
- 3 (6 inch) whole wheat pita breads
- 1 roma (plum) tomatoes, chopped
- 1/2 bunch spinach, rinsed and chopped
- 2 fresh mushrooms, sliced
- 1/4 cup crumbled feta cheese
- 1 tablespoon grated Parmesan cheese
- 1 tablespoon and 1-1/2 teaspoons olive oil
- ground black pepper to taste

Directions for Cooking:
1) Lightly grease baking pan of air fryer with cooking spray.
2) Evenly spread tomato pesto on one side of pita bread. Place one pita bread on bottom of pan, add 1/3 each of Parmesan, feta, mushrooms, spinach, and tomatoes. Season with pepper and drizzle with olive oil.
3) Cook for 5 minutes at 390ºF until tops crisped.
4) Repeat process for remaining pita bread.
5) Serve and enjoy.

Nutrition Information:
Calories: 367; Carbs: 41.6g; Protein: 11.6g; Fat: 17.1g

Chicken Deluxe Tetrazzini

(Servings: 3, Cooking Time: 30 minutes)

Ingredients:
- 4-ounce linguine pasta, cooked following manufacturer's Directions for Cooking:
- 2 tablespoons butter
- 3/4 cup sliced fresh mushrooms
- 1/4 cup minced onion
- 1/4 cup minced green bell pepper
- 1/2 (10.75 ounce) can condensed cream of mushroom soup
- 1/2 cup chicken broth
- 1/2 cup shredded sharp Cheddar cheese
- 1/4 (10 ounce) package frozen green peas
- 2 tablespoons cooking sherry
- 1/4 teaspoon Worcestershire sauce
- 1/4 teaspoon salt
- 1/8 teaspoon ground black pepper
- 1 cup chopped cooked chicken breast
- 1/4 cup grated Parmesan cheese

Directions for Cooking:
1) Lightly grease baking pan of air fryer and melt butter for 2 minutes at 360°F. Stir in bell pepper, onion, and mushrooms. Cook for 5 minutes.
2) Add chicken broth and mushroom soup, mix well. Cook for 5 minutes.
3) Mix in chicken, pepper, salt, Worcestershire sauce, sherry, peas, cheddar cheese, and pasta. Sprinkle paprika and Parmesan on top.
4) Cook for 15 minutes at 390°F until tops are lightly browned.
5) Serve and enjoy.

Nutrition Information:
Calories: 494; Carbs: 39.0g; Protein: 28.8g; Fat: 24.7g

Nutritious Cabbage Roll Bake

(Servings: 6, Cooking Time: 50 minutes)

Ingredients:
- 1-pound ground beef
- 1/2 cup chopped onion
- 1/2 (29 ounce) can tomato sauce
- 1-3/4 pounds chopped cabbage
- 1/2 cup uncooked white rice
- 1/2 teaspoon salt
- 1 (14 ounce) can beef broth

Directions for Cooking:
1) Lightly grease baking pan of air fryer with cooking spray. Add beef and for 10 minutes, cook on 360°F. Halfway through cooking time, stir and crumble beef.
2) Meanwhile, in a large bowl whisk well salt, rice, cabbage, onion, and tomato sauce. Add to pan of meat and mix well. Pour broth.
3) Cover pan with foil.
4) Cook for 25 minutes at 330°F, uncover, mix and cook for another 15 minutes.
5) Serve and enjoy.

Nutrition Information:
Calories: 356; Carbs: 25.5g; Protein: 17.1g; Fat: 20.6g

Vegan Approved Shepherd's Pie

(Servings: 3, Cooking Time: 35 minutes)

Top Layer Ingredients:
- 2-1/2 russet potatoes, peeled and cut into 1-inch cubes
- 1/4 cup vegan mayonnaise
- 1/4 cup soy milk
- 2 tablespoons olive oil
- 1 tablespoon and 1-1/2 teaspoons vegan cream cheese substitute (such as Tofutti ®)
- 1 teaspoon salt

Bottom Layer Ingredients:
- 1-1/2 teaspoons vegetable oil
- 1/2 large yellow onion, chopped
- 1 carrot, chopped
- 1-1/2 stalks celery, chopped
- 1/4 cup frozen peas
- 1/2 tomato, chopped
- 1/2 teaspoon Italian seasoning
- 1/2 clove garlic, minced, or more to taste
- 1/2 pinch ground black pepper to taste
- 1/2 (14 ounce) package vegetarian ground beef substitute
- 1/4 cup shredded Cheddar-style soy cheese

Directions for Cooking:
1) Boil potatoes until tender. Drain and transfer to a bowl. Mash potatoes with salt, vegan cream cheese, olive oil, soy milk, and vegan mayonnaise. Mix well until smooth. Set aside.
2) Lightly grease baking pan of air fryer with cooking spray. Add carrot, celery, onions, tomato, and peas. For 10 minutes, cook on 360°F. Stirring halfway through cooking time.
3) Stir in pepper, garlic, and Italian seasoning.
4) Stir in vegetarian ground beef substitute. Cook for 5 minutes while halfway through cooking time crumbling and mixing the beef substitute.
5) Evenly spread the beef and veggie mixture in pan. Top evenly with mashed potato mixture.
6) Cook for another 20 minutes or until mashed potatoes are lightly browned.
7) Serve and enjoy.

Nutrition Information:
Calories: 559; Carbs: 64.5g; Protein: 20.2g; Fat: 24.4g

Enchilada Leftovers Casserole

(Servings: 3, Cooking Time: 45 minutes)

Ingredients:
- 1/2 (15 ounce) can tomato sauce
- 2 tablespoons water
- 1/2 envelope taco seasoning mix
- 2-1/4 teaspoons chili powder
- 1-1/2 teaspoons vegetable oil
- 1/2-pound chicken breast tenderloins
- 1/2 (15 ounce) can black beans, drained
- 2 tablespoons cream cheese
- 1/2 cup shredded Mexican-style cheese blend, or more to taste
- 1/2 (7.5 ounce) package corn bread mix
- 1 egg

- 3 tablespoons milk

Directions for Cooking:
1) Lightly grease baking pan of air fryer with vegetable oil. Add chicken and cook for 5 minutes per side at 360°F.
2) Stir in chili powder, taco seasoning mix, water, and tomato sauce. Cook for 10 minutes, while stirring and turning chicken halfway through cooking time.
3) Remove chicken from pan and shred with two forks. Return to pan and stir in cream cheese and black beans. Mix well.
4) Top with Mexican cheese.
5) In a bowl, whisk well egg and milk. Add corn bread mix and mix well. Pour over chicken.
6) Cover pan with foil.
7) Cook for another 15 minutes. Remove foil and cook for 10 minutes more or until topping is lightly browned.
8) Let it rest for 5 minutes.
9) Serve and enjoy.

Nutrition Information:
Calories: 487; Carbs: 45.9g; Protein: 31.2g; Fat: 19.8g

Rice, Chicken 'n Salsa Casserole

(Servings: 4, Cooking Time: 65 minutes)

Ingredients:
- 2/3 cup uncooked white rice
- 1-1/3 cups water
- 2 skinless, boneless chicken breast halves
- 1 cup shredded Monterey Jack cheese
- 1 cup shredded Cheddar cheese
- 1/2 (10.75 ounce) can condensed cream of chicken soup
- 1/2 (10.75 ounce) can condensed cream of mushroom soup
- 1/2 onion, chopped
- 3/4 cup mild salsa

Directions for Cooking:
1) Lightly grease baking pan of air fryer with cooking spray. Add water, rice, and chicken. Cover with foil and for 25 minutes, cook on 360°F.
2) Remove foil and remove chicken and cut into bite sized pieces. Fluff rice and transfer to plate.
3) In a bowl mix well, cheeses. In another bowl whisk well salsa, onion, cream of mushroom, and cream of chicken.
4) In same air fryer baking pan evenly spread ½ of rice on bottom, top with ½ of chicken, ½ of soup mixture, and then ½ of cheese. Repeat layering process.
5) Cover with foil and cook for another 25 minutes. Remove foil and cook until top is browned, around 15 minutes.
6) Serve and enjoy.

Nutrition Information:
Calories: 475; Carbs: 34.8g; Protein: 30.0g; Fat: 23.9g

Veggie-Pasta 'n chicken Bake

(Servings: 3, Cooking Time: 30 minutes)

Ingredients:
- 1/2 cup dry fusilli pasta, cooked according to manufacturer's Directions for Cooking:
- 1 tablespoon and 1-1/2 teaspoons olive oil
- 3 chicken tenderloins, cut into chunks
- 1-1/2 teaspoons dried minced onion
- salt and pepper to taste
- garlic powder to taste
- 1-1/2 teaspoons dried basil
- 1-1/2 teaspoons dried parsley
- 1/2 (10.75 ounce) can condensed cream of chicken soup
- 1/2 (10.75 ounce) can condensed cream of mushroom soup
- 1 cup frozen mixed vegetables
- 1/2 cup dry bread crumbs
- 1 tablespoon grated Parmesan cheese
- 1 tablespoon butter, melted

Directions for Cooking:
1) Lightly grease baking pan of air fryer with oil. Add chicken and season with parsley, basil, garlic powder, pepper, salt, and minced onion. For 10 minutes, cook on 360°F. Stirring halfway through cooking time.
2) Then stir in mixed vegetables, mushroom soup, chicken soup, and cooked pasta. Mix well.
3) Mix well butter, Parmesan cheese, and bread crumbs in a small bowl and spread on top of casserole.

4) Cook for 20 minutes or until tops are lightly browned.
5) Serve and enjoy.

Nutrition Information:
Calories: 399; Carbs: 35.4g; Protein: 19.8g; Fat: 19.8g

Yummy Mac 'n Cheese

(Servings: 3, Cooking Time: 32 minutes)

Ingredients:
- 8-ounce elbow macaroni, cooked according to package Directions for Cooking:
- 2 tablespoons butter
- 2 tablespoons all-purpose flour
- 1/8 teaspoon dried thyme
- 1/8 teaspoon cayenne pepper
- 1/8 teaspoon white pepper
- 1-1/2 cups milk
- 1/2 pinch ground nutmeg
- 1/8 teaspoon Worcestershire sauce
- 1/2 teaspoon salt
- 1-1/2 cups shredded sharp Cheddar cheese, divided
- 1/2 teaspoon Dijon mustard
- 1/4 cup panko bread crumbs
- 1-1/2 teaspoons butter, melted

Directions for Cooking:
1) Melt 2 tbsp butter in baking pan of air fryer for 2 minutes at 360°F. Stir in flour and cook for 3 minutes, stirring every now and then. Stir in white pepper, cayenne pepper, and thyme. Cook for 2 minutes. Stir in a cup of milk and whisk well. Cook for 5 minutes while mixing constantly.
2) Mix in salt, Worcestershire sauce, and nutmeg . Mix well. Cook for 5 minutes or until thickened while stirring frequently.
3) Add cheese and mix well. Cook for 3 minutes or until melted and thoroughly mixed.
4) Stir in Dijon mustard and mix well. Add macaroni and toss well to coat. Sprinkle remaining cheese on top.
5) In a small bowl mix well 1 ½ tsp butter and panko. Sprinkle on top of cheese.
6) Cook for 15 minutes at 390°F until tops are lightly browned.
7) Serve and enjoy.

Nutrition Information:
Calories: 700; Carbs: 72.8g; Protein: 29.4g; Fat: 32.3g

Black Bean and Brown Rice Bake

(Servings: 4, Cooking Time: 62 minutes)

Ingredients:
- 3 tablespoons brown rice
- 1/2 cup vegetable broth
- 1-1/2 teaspoons olive oil
- 2 tablespoons and 2 teaspoons diced onion
- 1/2 medium zucchini, thinly sliced
- 1 cooked skinless boneless chicken breast halves, chopped
- 1/4 cup sliced mushrooms
- 1/4 teaspoon cumin
- salt to taste
- ground cayenne pepper to taste
- 1/2 (15 ounce) can black beans, drained
- 1/2 (4 ounce) can diced green chile peppers, drained
- 3 tablespoons shredded carrots
- 1 cup shredded Swiss cheese

Directions for Cooking:
1) Lightly grease baking pan of air fryer with cooking spray. Add rice and broth. Cover pan with foil cook for 10 minutes at 390°F. Lower heat to 300°F and fluff rice. Cook for another 10 minutes. Let it stand for 10 minutes and transfer to a bowl and set aside.
2) Add oil to same baking pan. Stir in onion and cook for 5 minutes at 330°F.
3) Stir in mushrooms, chicken, and zucchini. Mix well and cook for 5 minutes.
4) Stir in cayenne pepper, salt, and cumin. Mix well and cook for another 2 minutes.
5) Stir in ½ of the Swiss cheese, carrots, chiles, beans, and rice. Toss well to mix. Evenly spread in pan. Top with remaining cheese.
6) Cover pan with foil.
7) Cook for 15 minutes at 390°F and then remove foil and cook for another 5 to 10 minutes or until tops are lightly browned.
8) Serve and enjoy.

Nutrition Information:
Calories: 337; Carbs: 11.5g; Protein: 25.3g; Fat: 21.0g

Herb and Zucchini Bake

(Servings: 3, Cooking Time: 52 minutes)

Ingredients:
- 3 tablespoons uncooked long grain white rice
- 1/3 cup water
- 1 tablespoon vegetable oil
- 3/4-pound zucchini, cubed
- 1/2 cup sliced green onions
- 1/2 clove garlic, minced
- 1/2 teaspoon garlic salt
- 1/4 teaspoon basil
- 1/4 teaspoon sweet paprika
- 1/4 teaspoon dried oregano
- 3/4 cup seeded, chopped tomatoes
- 1 cup shredded sharp Cheddar cheese, divided

Directions for Cooking:
1) Lightly grease baking pan of air fryer with cooking spray. Add rice and water. Cover pan with foil cook for 10

minutes at 390°F. Lower heat to 300°F and fluff rice. Cook for another 10 minutes. Let it stand for 10 minutes and transfer to a bowl and set aside.
2) Add oil to same air fryer baking pan and add garlic, green onions, and zucchini. For 5 minutes, cook on 360°F. Halfway through cooking time, stir veggies.
3) Season with oregano, paprika, basil, and garlic salt. Cook for 2 minutes.
4) Add half cup cheese, tomatoes, and the cooked rice. Toss well to mix. Cook for 5 minutes.
5) Sprinkle remaining cheese on top.
6) Cook for 10 minutes at 390°F until tops are lightly browned.
7) Serve and enjoy.

Nutrition Information:
Calories: 274; Carbs: 16.5g; Protein: 12.4g; Fat: 17.5g

Lobster Lasagna Maine Style

(Servings: 6, Cooking Time: 50 minutes)

Ingredients:
- 1/2 (15 ounce) container ricotta cheese
- 1 egg
- 1 cup shredded Cheddar cheese
- 1/2 cup shredded mozzarella cheese
- 1/2 cup grated Parmesan cheese
- 1/2 medium onion, minced
- 1-1/2 teaspoons minced garlic
- 1 tablespoon chopped fresh parsley
- 1/2 teaspoon freshly ground black pepper
- 1 (16 ounce) jar Alfredo pasta sauce
- 8 no-boil lasagna noodles
- 1 pound cooked and cubed lobster meat
- 5-ounce package baby spinach leaves

Directions for Cooking:
1) Mix well half of Parmesan, half of mozzarella, half of cheddar, egg, and ricotta cheese in a medium bowl. Stir in pepper, parsley, garlic, and onion.
2) Lightly grease baking pan of air fryer with cooking spray.
3) On bottom of pan, spread ½ of the Alfredo sauce, top with a single layer of lasagna noodles. Followed by 1/3 of lobster meat, 1/3 of ricotta cheese mixture, 1/3 of spinach. Repeat layering process until all Ingredients: are used up.
4) Sprinkle remaining cheese on top. Shake pan to settle lasagna and burst bubbles. Cover pan with foil.
5) For 30 minutes, cook on 360°F.
6) Remove foil and cook for 10 minutes at 390°F until tops are lightly browned.
7) Let it stand for 10 minutes.
8) Serve and enjoy.

Nutrition Information:
Calories: 558; Carbs: 20.4g; Protein: 36.8g; Fat: 36.5g

Rice and Tuna Puff

(Servings: 6, Cooking Time: 60 minutes)

Ingredients:
- 2/3 cup uncooked white rice
- 1 1/3 cups water
- 1/3 cup butter
- 1/4 cup all-purpose flour
- 1 teaspoon salt
- 1/4 teaspoon ground black pepper
- 1 1/2 cups milk
- 2 egg yolks1 (12 ounce) can tuna, undrained
- 2 tablespoons grated onion
- 1 tablespoon lemon juice
- 2 egg whites

Directions for Cooking:
1) In a saucepan bring water to a boil. Stir in rice, cover and cook on low fire until liquid is fully absorbed, around 20 minutes.
2) In another saucepan over medium fire, melt butter. Stir in pepper, salt, and flour. Cook for 2 minutes. Whisking constantly, slowly add milk. Continue cooking and stirring until thickened.
3) In medium bowl, whisk egg yolks. Slowly whisk in half of the thickened milk mixture. Add to pan of remaining milk and continue cooking and stirring for 2 more minutes. Stir in lemon juice, onion, tuna, and rice.
4) Lightly grease baking pan of air fryer with cooking spray. And transfer rice mixture.
5) Beat egg whites until stiff peak forms. Slowly fold into rice mixture.
6) Cover pan with foil.
7) For 20 minutes, cook on 360°F.
8) Cook for 15 minutes at 390°F until tops are lightly browned and the middle has set.
9) Serve and enjoy.

Nutrition Information:
Calories: 302; Carbs: 24.1g; Protein: 20.6g; Fat: 13.6g

Yellow Squash Bake, Low Carb

(Servings: 4, Cooking Time: 30 minutes)

Ingredients:
- 1-1/2 teaspoons olive oil
- 1/2 teaspoon butter
- 1/2 small onion, chopped
- 1 clove garlic, minced
- 2 cups peeled and cubed yellow squash
- 1/2 teaspoon kosher salt
- 1/4 teaspoon freshly ground black pepper
- 2 tablespoons and 2 teaspoons finely chopped raw almonds
- 1/2 cup shredded Colby-Monterey Jack cheese, divided
- 1/4 cup heavy whipping cream
- 1 egg
- 3 tablespoons coarsely chopped roasted, salted almonds

Directions for Cooking:
1) Lightly grease baking pan of air fryer with cooking spray. Add garlic and onion. For 5 minutes, cook on 360°F. Halfway through cooking time, stir pan.

2) Stir in pepper, salt, and squash. Cook for another 8 minutes.
3) Mix in half of cheese and raw almonds.
4) In a small bowl, whisk well eggs and cream. Pour into pan and mix well.
5) Evenly spread squash and top with cheese and roasted almonds.
6) Cook for 15 minutes at 360°F until tops are lightly browned.
7) Serve and enjoy.

Nutrition Information:
Calories: 238; Carbs: 6.7g; Protein: 8.6g; Fat: 19.6g

Eggplant-Parm Bake

(Servings: 3, Cooking Time: 45 minutes)

Ingredients:
- 1 large eggplants
- 1 tablespoon olive oil
- 1/2 pinch salt, or as needed
- 1-1/2 teaspoons olive oil
- 1 clove garlic, sliced
- 1/4 teaspoon red pepper flakes
- 1-1/2 cups prepared marinara sauce
- 1/4 cup water, plus more as needed
- 1/4 cup and 2 tablespoons ricotta cheese
- 1/4 cup grated Parmesan cheese
- 2 tablespoons shredded pepper jack cheese
- salt and freshly ground black pepper to taste
- 1/4 cup and 2 tablespoons dry bread crumbs
- 1/4 cup grated Parmesan cheese
- 1 tablespoon olive oil

Directions for Cooking:
1) Cut eggplant crosswise in 5 pieces. Peel and chop two pieces into ½-inch cubes.
2) Lightly grease baking pan of air fryer with 1 tbsp olive oil. For 5 minutes, heat oil at 390°F. Add half eggplant strips and cook for 2 minutes per side. Transfer to a plate.
3) Add 1 ½ tsp olive oil and add garlic. Cook for a minute. Add chopped eggplants. Season with pepper flakes and salt. Cook for 4 minutes. Lower heat to 330°F and continue cooking eggplants until soft, around 8 minutes more.
4) Stir in water and marinara sauce. Cook for 7 minutes until heated through. Stirring every now and then. Transfer to a bowl.
5) In a bowl, whisk well pepper, salt, pepper jack cheese, Parmesan cheese, and ricotta. Evenly spread cheeses over eggplant strips and then fold in half.
6) Lay folded eggplant in baking pan. Pour marinara sauce on top.
7) In a small bowl whisk well olive oil, and bread crumbs. Sprinkle all over sauce.
8) Cook for 15 minutes at 390°F until tops are lightly browned.
9) Serve and enjoy.

Nutrition Information:
Calories: 405; Carbs: 41.1g; Protein: 12.7g; Fat: 21.4g

Seven Layers of Tortilla Pie

(Servings: 6, Cooking Time: 30 minutes)

Ingredients:
- 2 (15 ounce) cans pinto beans, drained and rinsed
- 1 cup salsa, divided
- 2 cloves garlic, minced
- 2 tablespoons chopped fresh cilantro
- 1 (15 ounce) can black beans, rinsed and drained
- 1/2 cup chopped tomatoes
- 7 (8 inch) flour tortillas
- 2 cups shredded reduced-fat Cheddar cheese
- 1 cup salsa
- 1/2 cup sour cream

Directions for Cooking:
1) Mash pinto beans in a large bowl and mix in garlic and salsa.
2) In another bowl whisk together tomatoes, black beans, cilantro, and ¼ cup salsa.
3) Lightly grease baking pan of air fryer with cooking spray. Spread 1 tortilla, spread ¾ cup pinto bean mixture evenly up to ½-inch away from the edge of tortilla, spread ¼ cup cheese on top. Cover with another tortilla, spread 2/3 cup black bean mixture, and then ¼ cup cheese. Repeat twice the layering process. Cover with the last tortilla, top with pinto bean mixture and then cheese.
4) Cover pan with foil.
5) Cook for 25 minutes at 390°F, remove foil and cook for 5 minutes or until tops are lightly browned.
6) Serve and enjoy.

Nutrition Information:
Calories: 409; Carbs: 54.8g; Protein: 21.1g; Fat: 11.7g

Penne Pasta 'n Portobello Bake

(Servings: 4, Cooking Time: 30 minutes)

Ingredients:
- 4-ounce penne pasta, cooked according to manufacturer's Directions for Cooking:
- 1 tablespoon vegetable oil
- 1/4-pound portobello mushrooms, thinly sliced
- 1/4 cup margarine
- 2 tablespoons all-purpose flour
- 1 large clove garlic, minced
- 1/4 teaspoon dried basil
- 1 cup milk
- 1 cup shredded mozzarella cheese
- 5-ounce frozen chopped spinach, thawed
- 2 tablespoons soy sauce

Directions for Cooking:
1) Lightly grease baking pan of air fryer with oil. For 2 minutes, heat on 360°F. Add mushrooms and cook for a minute. Transfer to a plate.
2) In same pan, melt margarine for a minute. Stir in basil, garlic, and flour. Cook for 3 minutes. Stir and cook for another 2 minutes. Stir in half of milk slowly while whisking continuously. Cook for another 2 minutes. Mix well. Cook for another 2 minutes. Stir in remaining milk and cook for another 3 minutes.

3) Add cheese and mix well.
4) Stir in soy sauce, spinach, mushrooms, and pasta. Mix well. Top with remaining cheese.
5) Cook for 15 minutes at 390°F until tops are lightly browned.
6) Serve and enjoy.

Nutrition Information:
Calories: 482; Carbs: 32.1g; Protein: 16.0g; Fat: 32.1g

Southwest Style Meaty Casserole

(Servings: 6, Cooking Time: 45 minutes)

Ingredients:
- 1 cup uncooked elbow macaroni, cooked according to manufacturer's instructions
- 1-pound ground beef
- 1 large onion, chopped
- 2 garlic cloves, minced
- 1 can (14-1/2 ounces each) diced tomatoes, undrained
- 1/2 can (16 ounces) kidney beans, rinsed and drained
- 1/2 can (6 ounces) tomato paste
- 1/2 can (4 ounces) chopped green chilies, drained
- 1 teaspoons salt
- 1 teaspoon chili powder
- 1/2 teaspoon ground cumin
- 1/2 teaspoon pepper
- 1 cup shredded Monterey Jack cheese
- 1 jalapeno pepper, seeded and chopped

Directions for Cooking:
1) Lightly grease baking pan of air fryer with cooking spray. Add ground beef, onion, and garlic. For 10 minutes, cook on 360°F. Halfway through cooking time, stir and crumble beef.
2) Mix in diced tomatoes, kidney beans, tomato paste, green chilies, salt, chili powder, cumin, and pepper. Mix well. Cook for another 10 minutes.
3) Stir in macaroni and mix well. Top with jalapenos and cheese.
4) Cover pan with foil.
5) Cook for 15 minutes at 390°F, remove foil and continue cooking for another 10 minutes until tops are lightly browned.
6) Serve and enjoy.

Nutrition Information:
Calories: 323; Carbs: 23.0g; Protein: 24.0g; Fat: 15.0g

Easy-Bake Spanish Rice

(Servings: 3, Cooking Time: 50 minutes)

Ingredients:
- 1/2-pound lean ground beef
- 1/4 cup finely chopped onion
- 2 tablespoons chopped green bell pepper
- 1/2 (14.5 ounce) can canned tomatoes
- 1/2 cup water
- 1/3 cup uncooked long grain rice
- 1/4 cup chile sauce
- 1/2 teaspoon salt
- 1/2 teaspoon brown sugar
- 1/4 teaspoon ground cumin
- 1/4 teaspoon Worcestershire sauce
- 1/2 pinch ground black pepper
- 1/4 cup shredded Cheddar cheese
- 1 tablespoon chopped fresh cilantro

Directions for Cooking:
1) Lightly grease baking pan of air fryer with cooking spray. Add ground beef. For 10 minutes, cook on 360°F. Halfway through cooking time, stir and crumble beef. Discard excess fat,
2) Stir in pepper, Worcestershire sauce, cumin, brown sugar, salt, chile sauce, rice, water, tomatoes, green bell pepper, and onion. Mix well. Cover pan with foil and cook for 25 minutes. Stirring occasionally.
3) Give it one last good stir, press down firmly and sprinkle cheese on top.
4) Cook uncovered for 15 minutes at 390°F until tops are lightly browned.
5) Serve and enjoy with chopped cilantro.

Nutrition Information:
Calories: 346; Carbs: 24.9g; Protein: 18.5g; Fat: 19.1g

Brown Rice 'n Chicken Curry Casserole

(Servings: 3, Cooking Time: 45 minutes)

Ingredients:
- 1/2 cup water
- 1/2 (8 ounce) can stewed tomatoes
- 1/4 cup and 2 tablespoons quick-cooking brown rice
- 1/4 cup raisins
- 1-1/2 teaspoons lemon juice
- 1-1/2 teaspoons curry powder
- 1/2 cube chicken bouillon
- 1/4 teaspoon ground cinnamon
- 1/8 teaspoon salt
- 1 clove garlic, minced
- 1/2 bay leaf (optional)
- 6 ounces skinless, boneless chicken breast halves - cut into 1-inch cubes

Directions for Cooking:
1) Lightly grease baking pan of air fryer with cooking spray.
2) Stir in bay leaf, garlic, salt, cinnamon, bouillon, curry powder, lemon juice, raisins, brown rice, stewed tomatoes, and water. For 20 minutes, cook on 360°F. Halfway through cooking time, stir in chicken and mix well.
3) Cover pan with foil.
4) Cook for 15 minutes at 390°F, remove foil, cook for 10 minutes until tops are lightly browned.
5) Serve and enjoy.

Nutrition Information:
Calories: 247; Carbs: 34.5g; Protein: 22.7g; Fat: 2.0g

Grilled Poultry Recipes

Rotisserie Chicken with Herbes De Provence

(Servings: 6, Cooking Time: 1 hour)

Ingredients:
- 3 pounds chicken, whole
- 2 tablespoons dried herbes de Provence
- 1 tablespoon salt

Directions for Cooking:
1) Season the whole chicken with dried herbes de Provence and salt. Rub all the seasoning on the chicken including the cavity.
2) Preheat the air fryer at 375°F.
3) Place the grill pan accessory in the air fryer.
4) Place the chicken and grill for 1 hour.

Nutrition information:
Calories: 256; Carbs:1.1 g; Protein: 46.2g; Fat: 6.2g

Grilled Oregano Chicken

(Servings: 6, Cooking Time: 40 minutes)

Ingredients:
- 3 pounds chicken breasts
- 2 tablespoons oregano, chopped
- 4 cloves of garlic, minced
- 1 tablespoon grated lemon zest
- 2 tablespoons fresh lemon juice
- Salt and pepper to taste

Directions for Cooking:
1) Preheat the air fryer at 375°F.
2) Place the grill pan accessory in the air fryer.
3) Season the chicken with oregano, garlic, lemon zest, lemon juice, salt and pepper.
4) Grill for 40 minutes and flip every 10 minutes to cook evenly.

Nutrition information:
Calories: 398; Carbs: 1.9g; Protein: 47.5g; Fat: 21.2g

Honey Sriracha Chicken

(Servings: 4, Cooking Time: 40 minutes)

Ingredients:
- 3 tablespoons rice vinegar
- 2 tablespoons sriracha
- 1 tablespoon honey
- 1 teaspoon Dijon mustard
- 4 chicken breasts
- ½ teaspoon paprika
- ½ teaspoon garlic powder
- Salt and pepper to taste

Directions for Cooking:
1) Place all ingredients in a Ziploc bag and allow to marinate for at least 2 hours in the fridge.
2) Preheat the air fryer at 375°F.
3) Place the grill pan accessory in the air fryer.
4) Grill the chicken for at least 40 minutes and flip the chicken every 10 minutes for even cooking.

Nutrition information:
Calories: 525; Carbs: 6.1g; Protein: 60.8g; Fat: 26.9g

Tequila Glazed Chicken

(Servings: 6, Cooking Time: 40 minutes)

Ingredients:
- 2 tablespoons whole coriander seeds
- Salt and pepper to taste
- 3 pounds chicken breasts
- 1/3 cup orange juice
- ¼ cup tequila
- 2 tablespoons brown sugar
- 2 tablespoons honey
- 3 cloves of garlic, minced
- 1 shallot, minced

Directions for Cooking:
1) Place all ingredients in a Ziploc bag and allow to marinate for at least 2 hours in the fridge.
2) Preheat the air fryer at 375°F.
3) Place the grill pan accessory in the air fryer.
4) Grill the chicken for at least 40 minutes.
5) Flip the chicken every 10 minutes for even cooking.
6) Meanwhile, pour the marinade in a saucepan and simmer until the sauce thickens.
7) Brush the chicken with the glaze before serving.

Nutrition information:
Calories: 449; Carbs: 11.2g; Protein: 48.1g; Fat: 22.5g

Grilled Sambal Chicken

(Servings: 3, Cooking Time: 25 minutes)

Ingredients:
- ½ cup light brown sugar
- ½ cup rice vinegar
- 1/3 cup hot chili paste
- ¼ cup fish sauce
- ¼ cup sriracha
- 2 teaspoons grated and peeled ginger
- 1 ½ pounds chicken breasts, pounded

Directions for Cooking:
1) Place all ingredients in a Ziploc bag and allow to marinate for at least 2 hours in the fridge.
2) Preheat the air fryer at 375°F.
3) Place the grill pan accessory in the air fryer.
4) Grill the chicken for 25 minutes.
5) Flip the chicken every 10 minutes for even grilling.
6) Meanwhile, pour the marinade in a saucepan and heat over medium heat until the sauce thickens.
7) Before serving the chicken, brush with the sriracha glaze.

Nutrition information:
Calories: 434; Carbs: 5.4g; Protein: 49.3g; Fat: 21.8g

Smoked Chicken Wings

(Servings: 8, Cooking Time: 30 minutes)

Ingredients:
- 3 tablespoons paprika
- 4 teaspoons salt
- 1 tablespoon chili powder
- 1 tablespoon garlic powder
- 1 teaspoon chipotle chili powder
- 1 teaspoon mustard powder
- 4 pounds chicken wings
- ½ cup barbecue sauce
- 1 tablespoon liquid smoke seasoning

Directions for Cooking:
1) Place all ingredients in a Ziploc bag.
2) Allow to marinate for at least 2 hours in the fridge.
3) Preheat the air fryer at 375°F.
4) Place the grill pan accessory in the air fryer.
5) Grill the chicken for 30 minutes.
6) Flip the chicken every 10 minutes for even grilling.
7) Meanwhile, pour the marinade in a saucepan and heat over medium heat until the sauce thickens.
8) Before serving the chicken, brush with the glaze.

Nutrition information:
Calories: 353; Carbs: 10.8g; Protein: 50.7g; Fat: 8.6g

Sweet and Sour Grilled Chicken

(Servings: 6, Cooking Time: 40 minutes)

Ingredients:
- 6 chicken drumsticks
- 1 cup water
- ¼ cup tomato paste
- 1 cup soy sauce
- 1 cup white vinegar
- ¾ cup sugar
- ¾ cup minced onion
- ¼ cup minced garlic
- Salt and pepper to taste

Directions for Cooking:
1) Place all ingredients in a Ziploc bag
2) Allow to marinate for at least 2 hours in the fridge.
3) Preheat the air fryer at 375ºF.
4) Place the grill pan accessory in the air fryer.
5) Grill the chicken for 40 minutes.
6) Flip the chicken every 10 minutes for even grilling.
7) Meanwhile, pour the marinade in a saucepan and heat over medium flame until the sauce thickens.
8) Before serving the chicken, brush with the glaze.

Nutrition information:
Calories: 416; Carbs:29.6 g; Protein: 27.8g; Fat: 19.7g

Lemon Grilled Chicken Breasts

(Servings: 6, Cooking Time: 40 minutes)

Ingredients:
- 3 tablespoons fresh lemon juice
- 2 tablespoons olive oil
- 2 cloves of garlic, minced
- 6 boneless chicken breasts, halved
- Salt and pepper to taste

Directions for Cooking:
1) Place all ingredients in a Ziploc bag
2) Allow to marinate for at least 2 hours in the fridge.
3) Preheat the air fryer at 375ºF.
4) Place the grill pan accessory in the air fryer.
5) Grill for 40 minutes and make sure to flip the chicken every 10 minutes for even cooking.

Nutrition information:
Calories: 372; Carbs: 1.5g; Protein: 61.5g; Fat: 11.7g

Spicy Peach Glazed Grilled Chicken

(Servings: 4, Cooking Time: 40 minutes)

Ingredients:
- 2 cups peach preserves
- 2 pounds chicken thighs
- 3 tablespoons olive oil
- 2 tablespoons soy sauce
- 1 tablespoons Dijon mustard
- 1 tablespoon chili powder
- 1 tablespoon minced garlic
- 1 jalapeno chopped
- Salt and pepper to taste

Directions for Cooking:
1) Place all ingredients in a Ziploc bag and allow to rest in the fridge for at least 2 hours.
2) Preheat the air fryer at 375°F.
3) Place the grill pan accessory in the air fryer.
4) Grill for 40 minutes while flipping the chicken every 10 minutes.
5) Meanwhile, pour the marinade in a saucepan and allow to simmer for 5 minutes until the sauce thickens.
6) Brush the chicken with the glaze before serving.

Nutrition information:
Calories: 726; Carbs: 31.7g; Protein: 39.4g; Fat: 49.5g

Chinese Style Chicken

(Servings: 4, Cooking Time: 40 minutes)

Ingredients:
- 2 teaspoons brown sugar
- 1 ½ teaspoon five spice powder
- Salt and pepper to taste
- 2 chicken breasts, halved
- 3 ½ teaspoon grated ginger
- ¼ cup hoisin sauce
- 2 tablespoons rice vinegar
- 3 ½ teaspoons honey
- 1 ¼ teaspoons sesame oil
- 3 cucumbers, sliced

Directions for Cooking:
1) Place all ingredients, except for the cucumber, in a Ziploc bag.
2) Allow to rest in the fridge for at least 2 hours.
3) Preheat the air fryer at 375°F.
4) Place the grill pan accessory in the air fryer.
5) Grill for 40 minutes and make sure to flip the chicken often for even cooking.
6) Serve chicken with cucumber once cooked.

Nutrition information:
Calories:336; Carbs:16.7 g; Protein: 31.2g; Fat: 15.4g

Garlic Cilantro-Lime Chicken

(Servings: 4, Cooking Time: 40 minutes)

Ingredients:
- 4 chicken breasts, halved
- 1 tablespoon lime zest
- 1/3 cup fresh lime juice
- 2 tablespoons olive oil
- 1 ½ teaspoon honey
- 1 teaspoon liquid smoke
- 1/3 cup chopped cilantro
- 3 cloves of garlic, minced
- Salt and pepper to taste

Directions for Cooking:
1) Place all ingredients in a bowl and allow to marinate in the fridge for at least 2 hours.
2) Preheat the air fryer at 390°F.
3) Place the grill pan accessory in the air fryer.
4) Grill in the chicken for 40 minutes and make sure to flip the chicken every 10 minutes for even grilling.

Nutrition information:
Calories: 581; Carbs: 6.1g; Protein: 60.9g; Fat: 33.6g

Grilled Chicken Stuffed with Cheese

(Servings: 4, Cooking Time: 30 minutes)

Ingredients:
- 1 tablespoon creole seasoning
- 1 teaspoon garlic powder
- 1 teaspoon onion powder
- 4 chicken breasts, butterflied and pounded
- 4 slices pepper jack cheese
- 4 slices Colby cheese
- 1 tablespoon olive oil

Directions for Cooking:
1) Preheat the air fryer at 390°F.
2) Place the grill pan accessory in the air fryer.
3) Create the dry rub by mixing in a bowl the creole seasoning, garlic powder, and onion powder. Season with salt and pepper if desired.
4) Rub the seasoning on to the chicken.
5) Place the chicken on a working surface and place a slice each of pepper jack and Colby cheese.
6) Fold the chicken and secure the edges with toothpicks.
7) Brush chicken with olive oil.
8) Grill for 30 minutes and make sure to flip the meat every 10 minutes.

Nutrition information:
Calories:742 ; Carbs:5.4 g; Protein: 73.1g; Fat: 45.9g

Southwest Chicken Foil Packets

(Servings: 4, Cooking Time: 40 minutes)

Ingredients:
- 4 chicken breasts
- Salt and pepper to taste
- 1 cup corn kernels, frozen
- 1 cup commercial salsa
- 1 can black beans, rinsed and drained
- 4 teaspoons taco seasoning
- 1 cup Mexican cheese blend, shredded
- 1 cup cilantro, chopped
- 4 lime wedges

Directions for Cooking:
1) Preheat the air fryer at 390°F.
2) Place the grill pan accessory in the air fryer.
3) On a big aluminum foil, place the chicken breasts and season with salt and pepper to taste.
4) Add the corn, commercial salsa beans, and taco seasoning.
5) Close the foil and crimp the edges.
6) Place on the grill pan and cook for 40 minutes.
7) Before serving, top with cheese, cilantro and lime wedges.

Nutrition information:
Calories: 838; Carbs: 47.5g; Protein: 80.1g; Fat: 36.2g

Teriyaki Grilled Chicken

(Servings: 3, Cooking Time: 40 minutes)

Ingredients:
- ½ cup soy sauce
- ½ cup water
- 3 tablespoons brown sugar
- 3 tablespoon honey
- 3 cloves of garlic, minced
- 1 tablespoon minced ginger
- 1 tablespoons rice vinegar
- 3 tablespoons olive oil
- 1 ½ pounds boneless skinless chicken breasts

Directions for Cooking:
1) Place all ingredients in a Ziploc bag and give a good shake. Allow to marinate in the fridge for at least 2 hours.
2) Preheat the air fryer at 390°F.
3) Place the grill pan accessory in the air fryer.
4) Grill the chicken for 40 minutes making sure to flip the chicken every 10 minutes.
5) Meanwhile, prepare the teriyaki glaze by pouring the marinade on a saucepan and allow to simmer over medium flame until the sauce thickens.
6) Before serving, brush the chicken with the teriyaki glaze.

Nutrition information:
Calories: 603; Carbs: 33.7g; Protein: 54.4g; Fat: 27.3g

Sweet and Spicy Grilled Chicken

(Servings: 4, Cooking Time: 35 minutes)

Ingredients:
- ½ cup brown sugar
- 2 tablespoons chili powder
- 1 teaspoon salt
- ½ teaspoon garlic powder
- 1 teaspoon liquid smoke seasoning
- 4 boneless chicken breasts

Directions for Cooking:
1) Place all ingredients in a Ziploc bag and give a good shake. Allow to marinate in the fridge for at least 2 hours.
2) Preheat the air fryer at 390°F.
3) Place the grill pan accessory in the air fryer.
4) Grill the chicken for 35 minutes.
5) Make sure to flip the chicken every 10 minute to grill evenly.

Nutrition information:
Calories: 446; Carbs: 29.6g; Protein: 61.8g; Fat: 7.7g

Hone, Lime, And Lime Grilled Chicken

(Servings: 4, Cooking Time: 40 minutes)

Ingredients:
- 2 pounds boneless chicken breasts
- ¼ cup lime juice, freshly squeezed
- ½ cup honey
- 2 tablespoons soy sauce
- 1 tablespoon olive oil
- 2 cloves of garlic, minced
- ½ cup cilantro, chopped finely
- Salt and pepper to taste

Directions for Cooking:
1) Place all ingredients in a Ziploc bag and give a good shake. Allow to marinate in the fridge for at least 2 hours.
2) Preheat the air fryer at 390°F.
3) Place the grill pan accessory in the air fryer.
4) Grill the chicken for 40 minutes making sure to flip the chicken every 10 minutes to grill evenly on all sides.

Nutrition information:
Calories:467 ; Carbs: 38.9g; Protein:52.5 g; Fat: 10.2g

Grilled Jerk Chicken

(Servings: 8, Cooking Time: 60 minutes)

Ingredients:
- 4 habanero chilies
- 5 cloves of garlic, minced
- ¾ malt vinegar
- ¾ soy sauce
- 2 tablespoons rum
- 2 tablespoon salt
- 2 ½ teaspoons ground allspice
- 1 ½ teaspoons ground nutmeg
- ¾ ground cloves
- 8 pieces chicken legs

Directions for Cooking:

1) Place all ingredients in a Ziploc bag and give a good shake. Allow to marinate in the fridge for at least 2 hours.
2) Preheat the air fryer at 390°F.
3) Place the grill pan accessory in the air fryer.
4) Grill the chicken for 60 minutes and flip the chicken every 10 minutes for even grilling.

Nutrition information:
Calories: 204; Carbs: 1.2g; Protein: 28.7 g; Fat: 8.1g

Butterflied Chicken with Herbs

(Servings: 4, Cooking Time: 1 hour)

Ingredients:
- 2 pounds whole chicken, backbones removed and butterflied
- Salt and pepper to taste
- 6 cloves of garlic, minced
- ¼ cup Aleppo-style pepper
- 1.4 cup chopped rosemary
- ¼ cup fresh lemon juice
- ¼ cup oregano
- 1 cup green olives, pitted and cracked

Directions for Cooking:

1) Place the chicken breast side up and slice through the breasts. Using your palms, press against the breastbone to flatten the breasts or you may remove the bones altogether.
2) Once the bones have been removed, season the chicken with salt, pepper, garlic, pepper, rosemary, lemon juice, and oregano.
3) Allow to marinate in the fridge for at least 12 hours.
4) Preheat the air fryer at 390°F.
5) Place the grill pan accessory in the air fryer.
6) Place the chicken on the grill pan and place the olives around the chicken.
7) Grill for 1 hour and make sure to flip the chicken every 10 minutes for even grilling.

Nutrition information:
Calories: 492; Carbs: 50.4 g; Protein: 37.6 g; Fat: 16.6g

4-Ingredient Garlic Herb Chicken Wings

(Servings: 4, Cooking Time: 35 minutes)

Ingredients:
- 2 pounds chicken wings
- 6 medium garlic cloves, grated
- ¼ cup chopped rosemary
- Salt and pepper to taste

Directions for Cooking:
1) Season the chicken with garlic, rosemary, salt and pepper.
2) Preheat the air fryer at 390°F.
3) Place the grill pan accessory in the air fryer.
4) Grill for 35 minutes and make sure to flip the chicken every 10 minutes.

Nutrition information:
Calories: 299 ; Carbs: 2.9g; Protein: 50.4g; Fat: 8.2g

Pesto Grilled Chicken

(Servings: 8, Cooking Time: 30 minutes)

Ingredients:
- 1 ¾ cup commercial pesto
- 8 chicken thighs
- Salt and pepper to taste

Directions for Cooking:
1) Place all ingredients in the Ziploc bag and allow to marinate in the fridge for at least 2 hours.
2) Preheat the air fryer at 390°F.
3) Place the grill pan accessory in the air fryer.
4) Grill the chicken for at least 30 minutes.
5) Make sure to flip the chicken every 10 minutes for even grilling.

Nutrition information:
Calories: 481; Carbs: 3.8g; Protein: 32.6g; Fat: 36.8g

Chili and Yogurt Marinated Chicken

(Servings: 3, Cooking Time: 40 minutes)

Ingredients:
- 7 dried chilies, seeds removed and broken into pieces
- 1-inch ginger, peeled and chopped
- 4 cloves of garlic, minced
- ½ cup whole milk yogurt
- 3 tablespoons fresh lime juice
- 2 tablespoons prepared mustard
- 1 tablespoon ground coriander
- 1 tablespoon smoked paprika
- 1 ½ teaspoon garam masala
- ½ teaspoon ground cumin
- 1 ½ pounds skinless chicken thighs
- Salt and pepper to taste

Directions for Cooking:
1) Place all ingredients in a Ziploc bag and give a good shake to combine everything.
2) Allow to marinate for at least 2 hours in the fridge.
3) Preheat the air fryer at 390°F.
4) Place the grill pan accessory in the air fryer.
5) Grill for at least 40 minutes.
6) Make sure to flip the chicken every 10 minutes.

Nutrition information:
Calories: 583; Carbs: 25.5g; Protein:54.6 g; Fat: 29.8g

Grilled Chicken with Board Dressing

(Servings: 8, Cooking Time: 40 minutes)

Ingredients:
- 1 dried Mexican chili, shredded
- ½ teaspoon crushed red pepper flakes
- ¾ cup fresh cilantro
- ¼ cup chopped oregano
- 1 teaspoon lime zest
- Salt and pepper to taste
- 4 pounds chicken breasts

Directions for Cooking:
1) Place all ingredients in a Ziploc bag and give a good shake.
2) Allow to marinate in the fridge for at least 2 hours.
3) Preheat the air fryer at 390°F.
4) Place the grill pan accessory in the air fryer.
5) Grill for at least 40 minutes making sure to flip the chicken every 10 minutes for even grilling.

Nutrition information:
Calories: 394; Carbs:0.9 g; Protein: 47.4g; Fat: 21g

Indian Spiced Chicken Eggplant and Tomato Skewers

(Servings: 4, Cooking Time: 25 minutes)

Ingredients:
- 4 cloves of garlic, minced
- 1-inch ginger, grated
- 1 can coconut milk
- 3 teaspoons lime zest
- 2 tablespoons fresh lime juice
- 2 tablespoons tomato paste
- Salt and pepper to taste
- 1 ½ teaspoon ground turmeric
- ¼ teaspoon cayenne pepper
- ¼ teaspoon ground cardamom
- 2 pounds boneless chicken breasts, cut into cubes
- 1 medium eggplant, cut into cubes
- 1 onion, cut into wedges
- 1 cup cherry tomatoes

Directions for Cooking:
1) Place in a bowl the garlic, ginger, coconut milk, lime zest, lime juice, tomato paste, salt, pepper, turmeric, cayenne pepper, cardamom, and chicken breasts. Allow to marinate in the fridge for at least for 2 hours.
2) Preheat the air fryer at 390°F.
3) Place the grill pan accessory in the air fryer.
4) Skewer the chicken cubes with eggplant, onion, and cherry tomatoes on bamboo skewers.
5) Place on the grill pan and cook for 25 minutes making sure to flip the chicken every 5 minutes for even cooking.

Nutrition information:
Calories: 479; Carbs:19.7 g; Protein: 55.2g; Fat: 20.6g

Easy Curry Grilled Chicken Wings

(Servings: 4, Cooking Time: 35 minutes)

Ingredients:
- 2 pounds chicken wings
- ½ cup plain yogurt
- 1 tablespoons curry powder
- Salt and pepper to taste

Directions for Cooking:
1) Season the chicken wings with yogurt, curry powder, salt and pepper. Toss to combine everything.
2) Allow to marinate in the fridge for at least 2 hours.
3) Preheat the air fryer at 390°F.
4) Place the grill pan accessory in the air fryer.
5) Grill the chicken for 35 minutes and make sure to flip the chicken halfway through the cooking time.

Nutrition information:
Calories:314 ; Carbs: 3.3g; Protein: 51.3g; Fat: 9.2g

Spicy Chicken with Lemon and Parsley in A Packet

(Servings: 4, Cooking Time: 45 minutes)

Ingredients:
- 2 pounds chicken thighs
- ¼ cup smoked paprika
- ½ teaspoon liquid smoke seasoning
- Salt and pepper to taste
- 1 ½ tablespoon cayenne pepper
- 4 lemons, halved
- ½ cup parsley leaves

Directions for Cooking:
1) Preheat the air fryer at 390°F.
2) Place the grill pan accessory in the air fryer.
3) In a large foil, place the chicken and season with paprika, liquid smoke seasoning, salt, pepper, and cayenne pepper.
4) Top with lemon and parsley.
5) Directions for Cooking:
6) Place on the grill and cook for 45 minutes.

Nutrition information:
Calories: 546; Carbs: 10.4g; Protein: 39.2g; Fat: 39.1g

Korean Grilled Chicken

(Servings: 4, Cooking Time: 30 minutes)

Ingredients:
- 2 pounds chicken wings
- 1 teaspoon salt
- ½ teaspoon fresh ground black pepper
- ½ cup gochujang
- 1 scallion, sliced thinly

Directions for Cooking:
1) Place in a Ziploc bag the chicken wings, salt, pepper, and gochujang sauce.
2) Allow to marinate in the fridge for at least 2 hours.
3) Preheat the air fryer at 390°F.
4) Place the grill pan accessory in the air fryer.
5) Grill the chicken wings for 30 minutes making sure to flip the chicken every 10 minutes.
6) Top with scallions and serve with more gochujang.

Nutrition information:
Calories: 289; Carbs: 0.8g; Protein: 50.1g; Fat: 8.2g

Grilled Chicken with Shishito Peppers

(Servings: 6, Cooking Time: 30 minutes)

Ingredients:
- 3 pounds chicken wings
- Salt and pepper to taste
- 2 tablespoons sesame oil
- 1 ½ cups shishito peppers, pureed

Directions for Cooking:
1) Place all ingredients in a Ziploc bowl and allow to marinate for at least 2 hours in the fridge.
2) Preheat the air fryer at 390°F.
3) Place the grill pan accessory in the air fryer.
4) Grill for at least 30 minutes flipping the chicken every 5 minutes and basting with the remaining sauce.

Nutrition information:
Calories: 333; Carbs: 1.7g; Protein: 50.2g; Fat: 12.6g

Grilled Chicken with Scallions

(Servings: 4, Cooking Time: 1 hour)

Ingredients:
- 2 pounds whole chicken
- Salt and pepper to taste
- 4 sprigs rosemary
- 2 heads of garlic, peeled and crushed
- 2 bunches scallions

Directions for Cooking:
1) Season the whole chicken with salt and pepper.
2) Place inside the chicken cavity the rosemary, garlic, and scallions.
3) Preheat the air fryer at 390°F.
4) Place the grill pan accessory in the air fryer.
5) Grill the chicken for 1 hour.

Nutrition information:
Calories: 470; Carbs: 46.2g; Protein: 37.2g; Fat: 15.9g

Piri Piri Chicken

(Servings: 6, Cooking Time: 45 minutes)

Ingredients:
- 3 pounds chicken breasts
- ½ cup piri piri sauce
- ¼ cup fresh lemon juice
- Salt and pepper to taste
- 1-inch fresh ginger, peeled and sliced thinly
- 1 large shallots, quartered
- 3 cloves of garlic, minced

Directions for Cooking:

1) Preheat the air fryer at 390°F.
2) Place the grill pan accessory in the air fryer.
3) On a large foil, place the chicken top with the rest of the ingredients.
4) Fold the foil and crimp the edges.
5) Grill for 45 minutes.

Nutrition information:
Calories:404 ; Carbs: 3.4g; Protein: 47.9g; Fat: 21.1g

Grilled Turmeric and Lemongrass Chicken

(Servings: 6, Cooking Time: 40 minutes)

Ingredients:
- 3 shallots, chopped
- 3 cloves of garlic, minced
- 2 lemongrass stalks
- 1 teaspoon turmeric
- Salt and pepper to taste
- 2 tablespoons fish sauce
- 3 pounds whole chicken

Directions for Cooking:

1) Place all ingredients in a Ziploc bag and allow to marinate for at least 2 hours in the fridge.
2) Preheat the air fryer at 390°F.
3) Place the grill pan accessory in the air fryer.
4) Grill the chicken for 40 minutes making sure to flip every 10 minutes for even grilling.

Nutrition information:
Calories: 486; Carbs: 49.1g; Protein: 38.5g; Fat: 16.1g

Peruvian Grilled Chicken

(Servings: 4, Cooking Time: 40 minutes)

Ingredients:
- 1/3 cup soy sauce
- 2 tablespoons fresh lime juice
- 5 cloves of garlic, minced
- 2 teaspoons ground cumin
- 1 teaspoon paprika
- ½ teaspoon dried oregano
- 2 ½ pounds chicken, quartered

Directions for Cooking:
1) Place all ingredients in a Ziploc bag and shake to mix everything.
2) Allow to marinate for at least 2 hours in the fridge.
3) Preheat the air fryer at 390°F.
4) Place the grill pan accessory in the air fryer.
5) Grill the chicken for 40 minutes making sure to flip the chicken every 10 minutes for even grilling.

Nutrition information:
Calories: 389 ; Carbs: 7.9g; Protein: 59.7g; Fat: 11.8g

Air Fryer Grilled Moroccan Chicken

(Servings: 4, Cooking Time: 40 minutes)

Ingredients:
- 2 pounds of boneless chicken thighs
- 4 cloves of garlic, chopped
- Salt and pepper to taste
- 2 teaspoons paprika
- ¼ teaspoons crushed red pepper flakes
- 2 teaspoons ground cumin

Directions for Cooking:
1) On a dish, season the chicken with garlic, salt, pepper, paprika, crushed red pepper flakes, and ground cumin.
2) Preheat the air fryer at 390°F.
3) Place the grill pan accessory in the air fryer.
4) Grill the chicken for 40 minutes.
5) Flip the chicken every 10 minutes to cook evenly.

Nutrition information:
Calories: 755; Carbs: 35.6g; Protein: 43.1g; Fat: 51.3g

Rotisserie Chicken with Herbes De Provence

(Servings: 6, Cooking Time: 1 hour)

Ingredients:
- 3 pounds chicken, whole
- 2 tablespoons dried herbes de Provence
- 1 tablespoon salt

Directions for Cooking:
1) Season the whole chicken with dried herbes de Provence and salt. Rub all the seasoning on the chicken including the cavity.
2) Preheat the air fryer at 390°F.
3) Place the grill pan accessory in the air fryer.
4) Place the chicken and grill for 1 hour.

Nutrition information:
Calories: 256; Carbs:1.1 g; Protein: 46.2g; Fat: 6.2g

Grilled Oregano Chicken

(Servings: 6, Cooking Time: 40 minutes)

Ingredients:
- 3 pounds chicken breasts
- 2 tablespoons oregano, chopped
- 4 cloves of garlic, minced
- 1 tablespoon grated lemon zest
- 2 tablespoons fresh lemon juice
- Salt and pepper to taste

Directions for Cooking:
1) Preheat the air fryer at 390°F.
2) Place the grill pan accessory in the air fryer.
3) Season the chicken with oregano, garlic, lemon zest, lemon juice, salt and pepper.
4) Grill for 40 minutes and flip every 10 minutes to cook evenly.

Nutrition information:
Calories: 398; Carbs: 1.9g; Protein: 47.5g; Fat: 21.2g

Honey Sriracha Chicken

(Servings: 4, Cooking Time: 40 minutes)

Ingredients:
- 3 tablespoons rice vinegar
- 2 tablespoons sriracha
- 1 tablespoon honey
- 1 teaspoon Dijon mustard
- 4 chicken breasts
- ½ teaspoon paprika
- ½ teaspoon garlic powder
- Salt and pepper to taste

Directions for Cooking:
1) Place all ingredients in a Ziploc bag and allow to marinate for at least 2 hours in the fridge.
2) Preheat the air fryer at 390°F.
3) Place the grill pan accessory in the air fryer.
4) Grill the chicken for at least 40 minutes and flip the chicken every 10 minutes for even cooking.

Nutrition information:
Calories: 525; Carbs: 6.1g; Protein: 60.8g; Fat: 26.9g

Tequila Glazed Chicken

(Servings: 6, Cooking Time: 40 minutes)

Ingredients:
- 2 tablespoons whole coriander seeds
- Salt and pepper to taste
- 3 pounds chicken breasts
- 1/3 cup orange juice
- ¼ cup tequila
- 2 tablespoons brown sugar
- 2 tablespoons honey
- 3 cloves of garlic, minced
- 1 shallot, minced

Directions for Cooking:
1) Place all ingredients in a Ziploc bag and allow to marinate for at least 2 hours in the fridge.
2) Preheat the air fryer at 390°F.
3) Place the grill pan accessory in the air fryer.
4) Grill the chicken for at least 40 minutes
5) Flip the chicken every 10 minutes for even cooking.
6) Meanwhile, pour the marinade in a saucepan and simmer until the sauce thickens.
7) Brush the chicken with the glaze before serving.

Nutrition information:
Calories: 449; Carbs: 11.2g; Protein: 48.1g; Fat: 22.5g

Grilled Sambal Chicken

(Servings: 3, Cooking Time: 25 minutes)

Ingredients:
- ½ cup light brown sugar
- ½ cup rice vinegar
- 1/3 cup hot chili paste
- ¼ cup fish sauce
- ¼ cup sriracha
- 2 teaspoons grated and peeled ginger
- 1 ½ pounds chicken breasts, pounded

Directions for Cooking:
1) Place all ingredients in a Ziploc bag and allow to marinate for at least 2 hours in the fridge.
2) Preheat the air fryer at 390°F.
3) Place the grill pan accessory in the air fryer.
4) Grill the chicken for 25 minutes.
5) Flip the chicken every 10 minutes for even grilling.
6) Meanwhile, pour the marinade in a saucepan and heat over medium flame until the sauce thickens.
7) Before serving the chicken, brush with the sriracha glaze.

Nutrition information:
Calories: 434; Carbs: 5.4g; Protein: 49.3g; Fat: 21.8g

Smoked Chicken Wings

(Servings: 8, Cooking Time: 30 minutes)

Ingredients:
- 3 tablespoons paprika
- 4 teaspoons salt
- 1 tablespoon chili powder
- 1 tablespoon garlic powder
- 1 teaspoon chipotle chili powder
- 1 teaspoon mustard powder
- 4 pounds chicken wings
- ½ cup barbecue sauce
- 1 tablespoon liquid smoke seasoning

Directions for Cooking:
1) Place all ingredients in a Ziploc bag
2) Allow to marinate for at least 2 hours in the fridge.
3) Preheat the air fryer at 390°F.
4) Place the grill pan accessory in the air fryer.
5) Grill the chicken for 30 minutes.
6) Flip the chicken every 10 minutes for even grilling.
7) Meanwhile, pour the marinade in a saucepan and heat over medium flame until the sauce thickens.
8) Before serving the chicken, brush with the glaze.

Nutrition information:
Calories: 353; Carbs: 10.8g; Protein: 50.7g; Fat: 8.6g

Sweet and Sour Grilled Chicken

(Servings: 6, Cooking Time: 40 minutes)

Ingredients:
- 6 chicken drumsticks
- 1 cup water
- ¼ cup tomato paste
- 1 cup soy sauce
- 1 cup white vinegar
- ¾ cup sugar
- ¾ cup minced onion
- ¼ cup minced garlic
- Salt and pepper to taste

Directions for Cooking:
1) Place all ingredients in a Ziploc bag
2) Allow to marinate for at least 2 hours in the fridge.
3) Preheat the air fryer at 390°F.
4) Place the grill pan accessory in the air fryer.
5) Grill the chicken for 40 minutes.
6) Flip the chicken every 10 minutes for even grilling.
7) Meanwhile, pour the marinade in a saucepan and heat over medium flame until the sauce thickens.
8) Before serving the chicken, brush with the glaze.

Nutrition information:
Calories: 416; Carbs:29.6 g; Protein: 27.8g; Fat: 19.7g

Lemon Grilled Chicken Breasts

(Servings: 6, Cooking Time: 40 minutes)

Ingredients:
- 3 tablespoons fresh lemon juice
- 2 tablespoons olive oil
- 2 cloves of garlic, minced
- 6 boneless chicken breasts, halved
- Salt and pepper to taste

Directions for Cooking:
1) Place all ingredients in a Ziploc bag
2) Allow to marinate for at least 2 hours in the fridge.
3) Preheat the air fryer at 390°F.
4) Place the grill pan accessory in the air fryer.
5) Grill for 40 minutes and make sure to flip the chicken every 10 minutes for even cooking.

Nutrition information:
Calories: 372; Carbs: 1.5g; Protein: 61.5g; Fat: 11.7g

Spicy Peach Glazed Grilled Chicken

(Servings: 4, Cooking Time: 40 minutes)

Ingredients:
- 2 cups peach preserves
- 2 pounds chicken thighs
- 3 tablespoons olive oil
- 2 tablespoons soy sauce
- 1 tablespoons Dijon mustard
- 1 tablespoon chili powder
- 1 tablespoon minced garlic
- 1 jalapeno chopped
- Salt and pepper to taste

Directions for Cooking:
1) Place all ingredients in a Ziploc bag and allow to rest in the fridge for at least 2 hours.
2) Preheat the air fryer at 390°F.
3) Place the grill pan accessory in the air fryer.
4) Grill for 40 minutes while flipping the chicken every 10 minutes.
5) Meanwhile, pour the marinade in a saucepan and allow to simmer for 5 minutes until the sauce thickens.
6) Brush the chicken with the glaze before serving.

Nutrition information:
Calories: 726; Carbs: 31.7g; Protein: 39.4g; Fat: 49.5g

Chinese Style Chicken

(Servings: 4, Cooking Time: 40 minutes)

Ingredients:
- 2 teaspoons brown sugar
- 1 ½ teaspoon five spice powder
- Salt and pepper to taste
- 2 chicken breasts, halved
- 3 ½ teaspoon grated ginger
- ¼ cup hoisin sauce
- 2 tablespoons rice vinegar
- 3 ½ teaspoons honey
- 1 ¼ teaspoons sesame oil
- 3 cucumbers, sliced

Directions for Cooking:
1) Place all ingredients except for the cucumber in a Ziploc bag.
2) Allow to rest in the fridge for at least 2 hours.
3) Preheat the air fryer at 390°F.
4) Place the grill pan accessory in the air fryer.
5) Grill for 40 minutes and make sure to flip the chicken often for even cooking.
6) Serve chicken with cucumber once cooked.

Nutrition information:
Calories:336 ; Carbs:16.7 g; Protein: 31.2g; Fat: 15.4g

Vegetable Recipes

Air Fried Grilled Asparagus

(Servings: 1, Cooking Time: 15 minutes)

Ingredients:
- ½ bunch asparagus spears, trimmed
- Salt and pepper to taste
- 1 tablespoon olive oil

Directions for Cooking:
1) Preheat the air fryer at 375°F.
2) Place the grill pan accessory in the air fryer.
3) Season the asparagus with salt and pepper. Drizzle with oil.
4) Place on the grill pan and cook for 15 minutes.
5) Give the air fryer a good shake to cook evenly.

Nutrition information:
Calories: 138; Carbs: 4.3g; Protein: 0.9g; Fat: 13.5g

Grilled Hasselback Potatoes

(Servings: 1, Cooking Time: 25 minutes)

Ingredients:
- 1 large potato
- 1 tablespoon butter
- ½ tablespoon oil
- Salt and pepper to taste

Directions for Cooking:
1) Preheat the air fryer at 375°F.
2) Place the grill pan accessory in the air fryer.
3) Place the potato on a cutting board. Place chopsticks on each side of the potato and slice until where the cut marks are.
4) Brush potato with butter and oil.
5) Season with salt and pepper to taste.
6) Place on the grill pan and cook for 20 to 25 minutes

Nutrition information:
Calories: 464; Carbs: 68.7g; Protein: 8.7g; Fat: 18.6g

Air Fryer Roasted Vegetables

(Servings: 4, Cooking Time: 15 minutes)

Ingredients:
- 1 teaspoon olive oil
- 1 bunch asparagus spears, trimmed
- 1 yellow squash, seeded and cut in circles
- 1 zucchini, seeded and cut in circles
- 1 cup button mushrooms, quartered
- Salt and pepper to taste
- 1 teaspoon basil powder
- 1 teaspoon thyme

Directions for Cooking:
1) Preheat the air fryer at 375°F.
2) Place the grill pan accessory in the air fryer.

3) Mix all vegetables in a bowl and toss to coat everything with the seasoning.
4) Place on the grill pan and cook for 15 minutes.
5) Make sure to stir the vegetables halfway through the cooking time.

Nutrition information:
Calories: 38; Carbs: 5.8g; Protein: 1.8g; Fat: 1.5g

Air Fried Roasted Summer Squash

(Servings: 2, Preparation Time: 5 minutes, Cooking Time: 15 minutes)

Ingredients:
- 1-pound zucchini, sliced into rounds or circles
- 2 tablespoons extra virgin olive oil
- 1 teaspoon salt
- ½ teaspoon black pepper
- 1 teaspoon garlic powder

Directions for Cooking:
1) Preheat the air fryer at 375°F.
2) Place the grill pan accessory in the air fryer.
3) In a mixing bowl, toss all Ingredients: until well-combined.
4) Place on the grill pan and cook for 15 minutes.
5) Stir the vegetables halfway through the cooking time.

Nutrition information:
Calories:109; Carbs: 8.6g; Protein: 6.9g; Fat: 6.5g

Grilled Cauliflower Bites

(Servings: 1, Cooking Time: 15 minutes)

Ingredients:
- 1 ½ cups cauliflower florets
- 1 tablespoon olive oil
- 2 tablespoons nutritional yeast
- Salt and pepper to taste

Directions for Cooking:
1) Preheat the air fryer at 375°F.
2) Place the grill pan accessory in the air fryer.
3) In a mixing bowl, toss all Ingredients: until well-combined.
4) Dump the vegetables on to the grill pan and cook for 10 to 15 minutes.

Nutrition information:
Calories: 81; Carbs: 6.5g; Protein: 4.2g; Fat: 4.9g

Roasted Air Fried Vegetables

(Servings: 4, Cooking Time: 15 minutes)

Ingredients:
- 12 small red potatoes, scrubbed and halved
- 1 cup chopped carrots
- 1 cup butternut squash, peeled and chopped
- 1 cup red onion, diced
- 1 red pepper, chopped
- 1 tablespoon olive oil
- 1 teaspoon thyme
- 1 teaspoon basil
- 1 teaspoon Italian seasoning
- ½ teaspoon garlic powder
- Salt and pepper to taste

Directions for Cooking:
1) Preheat the air fryer at 375°F.
2) Place the grill pan accessory in the air fryer.
3) In a mixing bowl, toss all Ingredients: until well-combined.
4) Place on the grill pan and cook for 15 minutes.
5) Stir the vegetables halfway through the cooking time to grill evenly.

Nutrition information:
Calories: 127; Carbs: 22.4g; Protein: 2.6g

Air Fryer Grilled Mexican Corn

(Servings: 4, Cooking Time: 15 minutes)

Ingredients:
- 4 pieces fresh corn on the cob
- ¼ teaspoon chili powder
- ½ teaspoon stone house seasoning
- ¼ cup chopped cilantro
- 1 lime cut into wedge
- ¼ cup cojita or feta cheese

Directions for Cooking:
1) Preheat the air fryer at 375°F.
2) Place the grill pan accessory in the air fryer.
3) Season the corn with chili powder and stone house seasoning.
4) Place on the grill pan and cook for 15 minutes while flipping the corn halfway through the cooking time.
5) Serve the corn with cilantro, lime, and feta cheese.

Nutrition information:
Calories:102; Carbs: 17g; Protein: 4g; Fat: 3g

Crispy and Spicy Grilled Broccoli in Air Fryer

(Servings: 1, Cooking Time: 15 minutes)

Ingredients:
- 1 head of broccoli, cut into florets
- 2 tablespoons yogurt
- 1 tablespoon chickpea flour
- Salt and pepper to taste
- ½ teaspoon red chili flakes
- 1 tablespoon nutritional yeast

Directions for Cooking:
1) Preheat the air fryer at 375°F.
2) Place the grill pan accessory in the air fryer.
3) Put all Ingredients in a Ziploc bag and shake until well combined.
4) Dump the Ingredients: on the grill pan and cook for 15 minutes until crispy.

Nutrition information:
Calories: 96; Carbs: 16.9g; Protein: 7.1g; Fat: 1.3g

Easy Grilled Corn in The Air Fryer

(Servings: 4, Cooking Time: 20 minutes)

Ingredients:
- 2 ears of corn
- Salt and pepper to taste
- 2 teaspoons vegetable oil

Directions for Cooking:
1) Preheat the air fryer at 375°F.
2) Place the grill pan accessory in the air fryer.
3) Season the corn with salt and pepper. Brush with oil.
4) Place on the grill pan and cook for 20 minutes making sure to flip the corn every 5 minutes to brown evenly.

Nutrition information:
Calories: 86; Carbs: 14.6g; Protein:2.5 g; Fat: 3.1g

Grilled Pineapple and Peppers

(Servings: 2, Cooking Time: 10 minutes)

Ingredients:
- 1 medium-sized pineapple, peeled and sliced
- 1 red bell pepper, seeded and julienned
- 2 teaspoons melted butter
- 1 teaspoon brown sugar
- Salt to taste

Directions for Cooking:
1) Preheat the air fryer at 390°F.
2) Place the grill pan accessory in the air fryer.
3) Mix all Ingredients: in a Ziploc bag and give a good shake.
4) Dump onto the grill pan and cook for 10 minutes making sure that you flip the pineapples every 5 minutes.

Nutrition information:
Calories:295; Carbs: 57g; Protein: 1g; Fat: 8g

Grilled Onion Potatoes

(Servings: 4, Cooking Time: 25 minutes)

Ingredients:
- 2 pounds baby red potatoes, scrubbed and halved
- 2 tablespoons olive oil
- 1 envelop onion soup mix

Directions for Cooking:
1) Preheat the air fryer at 390°F.
2) Place the grill pan accessory in the air fryer.
3) Mix all ingredients: in a Ziploc bag and give a good shake to coat the potatoes with the onion soup mix.
4) Dump on to the grill pan and cook for 20 to 25 minutes.
5) Make sure to give the potatoes a stir every 5 minutes to grill evenly.

Nutrition information:
Calories: 218; Carbs: 36.1g; Protein: 4.2g; Fat: 7.1g

Grilled Frozen Vegetables

(Servings: 4, Cooking Time: 35 minutes)

Ingredients:
- 2 bags frozen vegetable mix of your choice
- 1 tablespoon salt and pepper to taste
- 2 tablespoon coconut oil
- 2 tablespoon balsamic vinegar

Directions for Cooking:
1) Preheat the air fryer at 390°F.
2) Place the grill pan accessory in the air fryer.
3) Season the vegetables with salt, pepper, oil, and balsamic vinegar.
4) Dump the vegetables on the grill pan and cook for 35 minutes.
5) Give the grill pan a good shake to grill the vegetables evenly.

Nutrition information:
Calories: 160; Carbs: 20.5g; Protein: 4.2g; Fat: 7.1g

Simple Grilled Vegetables

(Servings: 4, Cooking Time: 20 minutes)

Ingredients:
- 1 tablespoon rosemary, chopped
- 1 clove of garlic, minced
- 1 tablespoon fresh basil, chopped
- 1 tablespoon fresh parsley
- 1 medium eggplant, sliced
- 1 zucchini, sliced
- 1 yellow squash, seeded and sliced
- 1 red onion, sliced
- Salt and pepper to taste
- 3 tablespoons nutritional yeast

Directions for Cooking:
1) Preheat the air fryer at 390°F.
2) Place the grill pan accessory in the air fryer.

3) Place all ingredients: in a bowl and toss the vegetables until all vegetables are seasoned well.
4) Dump the vegetables on to the grill pan and cook for 15 to 20 minutes.
5) Make sure to give the vegetables a shake to grill evenly on all sides.

Nutrition information:
Calories:68; Carbs: 12.6g; Protein: 5.1g; Fat: 0.5g

Italian Grilled Vegetables

(Servings: 4, Cooking Time:15 minutes)

Ingredients:
- 8-ounce baby bella mushrooms, sliced
- 12 ounces baby potatoes, scrubbed and halved
- 12 ounces cherry tomatoes, halved
- 2 zucchinis, sliced
- 12 garlic cloves, peeled and grated
- 2 tablespoon extra-virgin olive oil
- ½ tablespoon dried oregano
- 1 teaspoon dried thyme
- Salt and pepper to taste
- 3 tablespoons grated parmesan cheese
- A pinch of crushed red pepper flakes

Directions for Cooking:
1) Preheat the air fryer at 390°F.
2) Place the grill pan accessory in the air fryer.
3) Place all Ingredients: in a bowl and toss the vegetables until all vegetables are seasoned well.
4) Dump the seasoned vegetables on the grill pan and cook for 15 minutes.
5) Give a good shake every 5 minutes to evenly grill the vegetables.

Nutrition information:
Calories: 353; Carbs: 77g; Protein: 10.3g; Fat: 4.9g

Balsamic Grilled Vegetables

(Servings: 6, Cooking Time: 20 minutes)

Ingredients:
- 2 small zucchinis, sliced
- 1 yellow squash, seeded and sliced
- 1 large yellow onion, cut into rings
- 1 small head broccoli, cut into florets
- ½ head cauliflower, cut into florets
- 1 carrot, peeled and sliced
- Salt and pepper to taste
- ½ cup balsamic vinegar
- 2 tablespoons olive oil

Directions for Cooking:
1) Preheat the air fryer at 350°F.
2) Place the grill pan accessory in the air fryer.
3) Put all vegetables in a Ziploc bag and season with salt, pepper, balsamic vinegar, and olive oil.
4) Shake to season all vegetables.
5) Dump on to the grill pan and cook for 15 to 20 minutes.
6) Make sure to give the vegetables a good shake every 5 minutes.

Nutrition information:
Calories: 124; Carbs: 24g; Protein: 6g; Fat: 1g

Grilled Vegetables with Lemon Herb Vinaigrette

(Servings: 4, Cooking Time: 15 minutes)

Ingredients:
- 1 cup sliced carrots
- 1 zucchini, sliced
- 1 red bell pepper, seeded and julienned
- 1 cup snow peas
- Salt and pepper to taste
- 1 tablespoon olive oil
- 2 tablespoons nutritional yeast
- 1/8 cup red wine vinegar
- 1 teaspoon Dijon mustard
- 2 cloves of garlic, minced
- 1 tablespoon lemon juice
- 2 tablespoons honey

Directions for Cooking:
1) Preheat the air fryer at 350°F.
2) Place the grill pan accessory in the air fryer.
3) In a Ziploc bag, combine the carrots, zucchini, bell pepper, and snow peas. Season with salt, pepper, olive oil, and nutritional yeast. Give a good shake to combine everything.
4) Dump on to the grill pan and cook for 15 minutes.
5) Meanwhile, combine the red wine vinegar, Dijon mustard, garlic, lemon juice, and honey. Season with salt and pepper to taste.
6) Drizzle the grilled vegetables with the sauce.

Nutrition information:
Calories: 93; Carbs: 13.5g; Protein: 2.8g; Fat: 2.5g

Grilled Zucchini with Mozzarella

(Servings: 6, Cooking Time: 20 minutes)

Ingredients:
- 3 medium zucchinis, sliced lengthwise
- 3 tablespoons extra virgin olive oil
- Salt and ground black pepper
- 18-ounce mozzarella ball, pulled into large pieces
- 2 tablespoons fresh dill
- ¼ crushed red pepper
- 1 tablespoon lemon juice

Directions for Cooking:
1) Preheat the air fryer at 350°F.
2) Place the grill pan accessory in the air fryer.
3) Drizzle the zucchini with olive oil and season with salt and pepper to taste.
4) Place on the grill pan and cook for 15 to 20 minutes.
5) Serve the zucchini with mozzarella, dill, red pepper and lemon juice.

Nutrition information:
Calories:182; Carbs: 18.3g; Protein: 11.4g; Fat: 7.1g

Grilled Vegetables with Garlic

(Servings: 4, Cooking Time: 15 minutes)

Ingredients:
- 1 package frozen chopped vegetables
- 1 red onion, sliced
- 1 cup baby Portobello mushrooms, chopped
- Salt and pepper to taste
- 4 cloves of garlic, minced
- 3 tablespoon red wine vinegar
- ¼ cup chopped fresh basil
- 1 ½ tablespoons honey1 teaspoon Dijon mustard
- 1/3 cup olive oil

Directions for Cooking:
1) Preheat the air fryer at 350°F.
2) Place the grill pan accessory in the air fryer.
3) In a Ziploc bag, combine the vegetables and season with salt, pepper, and garlic. Give a good shake to combine everything.
4) Dump on to the grill pan and cook for 15 minutes.
5) Meanwhile, combine the rest of the Ingredients in a bowl and season with more salt and pepper.
6) Drizzle the grilled vegetables with the sauce. Serve and enjoy.

Nutrition information:
Calories: 200; Carbs: 8.3g; Protein: 2.1g; Fat: 18.2g

Grilled Tomato Melts

(Servings: 3, Cooking Time: 20 minutes)

Ingredients:
- 3 large tomatoes
- 4 ounces Monterey Jack cheese
- 1 yellow red bell pepper, chopped
- ¼ cup toasted almonds
- Salt and pepper to taste

Directions for Cooking:
1) Preheat the air fryer at 350°F.
2) Place the grill pan accessory in the air fryer.
3) Slice the tops of the tomatoes and remove the seeds to create hollow "cups."
4) In a mixing bowl, combine the cheese, bell pepper, and almonds. Season with salt and pepper to taste.
5) Stuff the tomatoes with the cheese filling.
6) Place the stuffed tomatoes on the grill pan and cook for 15 to 20 minutes.

Nutrition information:
Calories: 125; Carbs: 13g; Protein: 10g; Fat: 14g

Asparagus with Hollandaise Sauce

(Servings: 6, Cooking Time: 15 minutes)

Ingredients:
- 3 pounds asparagus spears, trimmed
- 2 tablespoons olive oil
- ½ teaspoon salt
- ¼ teaspoon black pepper
- 3 egg yolks
- ½ lemon juice
- ½ teaspoon salt
- A pinch of mustard powder
- A punch of ground white pepper
- ½ cup butter, melted
- 1 teaspoon chopped tarragon leaves

Directions for Cooking:
1) Preheat the air fryer at 350ºF.
2) Place the grill pan accessory in the air fryer.
3) In a Ziploc bag, combine the asparagus, olive oil, salt and pepper. Give a good shake to combine everything.
4) Dump on to the grill pan and cook for 15 minutes.
5) Meanwhile, on a double boiler over medium flame, whisk the egg yolks, lemon juice, and salt until silky. Add in the mustard powder, white pepper and melted butter. Keep whisking until the sauce is smooth. Garnish with tarragon leaves.
6) Drizzle the sauce over asparagus spears.

Nutrition information:
Calories: 253; Carbs: 10.2g; Protein: 6.7g; Fat: 22.4g

Air Fryer Grilled Mushrooms

(Servings: 2, Cooking Time: 20 minutes)

Ingredients:
- 6 large Portobello mushrooms, sliced
- ½ cup Italian vinaigrette
- ½ teaspoon black pepper
- 4 eggplants, sliced
- 4 onion, sliced
- 2 yellow bell peppers, seeded and sliced
- 5 ounces shredded mozzarella cheese

Directions for Cooking:
1) Preheat the air fryer at 350ºF.
2) Place the grill pan accessory in the air fryer.
3) In a Ziploc bag, put all Ingredients, except for the cheese. Shake to combine.
4) Dump on the grill pan and cook for 20 minutes.
5) While still hot, garnish with mozzarella cheese.

Nutrition information:
Calories: 212; Carbs: 23g; Protein: 13g; Fat: 14g

Grilled Asparagus and Arugula Salad

(Servings: 4, Cooking Time: 15 minutes)

Ingredients:
- 1-pound fresh asparagus, trimmed
- 2 tablespoons olive oil
- Salt and pepper to taste
- ¼ cup olive oil
- 2 teaspoons lemon zest
- 3 tablespoons lemon juice
- 3 tablespoons balsamic vinegar
- 4 cups arugula leaves
- 1 cup parmesan cheese, grated

Directions for Cooking:
1) Preheat the air fryer at 350°F.
2) Place the grill pan accessory in the air fryer.
3) In a Ziploc bag, combine the asparagus, olive oil, salt and pepper. Give a good shake to combine everything. Dump on to the grill pan and cook for 15 minutes.
4) Meanwhile, prepare the sauce by mixing together the olive oil, lemon, zest, lemon juice, and balsamic vinegar. Season with salt and pepper to taste. Set aside.
5) Assemble the salad by mixing the asparagus, arugula, and parmesan cheese. Drizzle with sauce on top.

Nutrition information:
Calories: 231; Carbs: 14g; Protein: 10g; Fat: 29g

Spicy Thai –Style Veggies

(Servings: 4, Cooking Time: 15 minutes)

Ingredients:
- 1 ½ cups packed cilantro leaves
- 8 cloves of garlic, minced
- 2 tablespoons fish sauce
- 1 tablespoon black pepper
- 1 tablespoon chili garlic sauce
- 1/3 cup vegetable oil
- 2 pounds vegetable of your choice, sliced into cubes

Directions for Cooking:
1) Preheat the air fryer at 350°F.
2) Place the grill pan accessory in the air fryer.
3) Place all ingredients: in a mixing bowl and toss to coat all ingredients.
4) Put in the grill pan and cook for 15 minutes.

Nutrition information:
Calories: 340; Carbs: 34.44g; Protein:8.8 g; Fat: 19.5g

Grilled Vegetables with Smokey Mustard Sauce

(Servings: 5, Cooking Time: 15 minutes)

Ingredients:
- 2 medium zucchinis, cut into ½ inch thick slices
- 2 large yellow squash, cut into ½ inch thick slices
- 1 large red bell pepper, sliced
- 3 tablespoons olive oil
- 1 teaspoon salt
- 1 teaspoon black pepper
- ¼ cup yellow mustard
- ¼ cup honey
- 2 teaspoons smoked paprika
- 2 teaspoons creole seasoning

Directions for Cooking:
1) Preheat the air fryer at 350ºF.
2) Place the grill pan accessory in the air fryer.
3) In a Ziploc bag, put the zucchini, squash, red bell pepper, olive oil, salt and pepper. Give a shake to season all vegetables.
4) Place on the grill pan and cook for 15 minutes.
5) Meanwhile, prepare the sauce by combining the mustard, honey, paprika, and creole seasoning. Season with salt to taste.
6) Serve the vegetables with the sauce.

Nutrition information:
Calories: 164; Carbs: 21.5g; Protein: 2.6g; Fat: 8.9g

Indian Grilled Vegetables

(Servings: 6, Cooking Time: 20 minutes)

Ingredients:
- ½ cup yogurt
- 6 cloves of garlic, minced
- 2-inch fresh ginger, minced
- 3 tablespoons Tandoori spice blend
- 2 tablespoons canola oil
- 2 small onions, cut into wedges
- 1 small zucchini, cut into thick slices
- 1 carrot, peeled and shaved to 1/8-inch thick
- 1 yellow sweet pepper, seeded and chopped
- ½ head cauliflower, cut into florets
- 1 handful sugar snap peas
- 1 cup young ears of corn

Directions for Cooking:
1) Preheat the air fryer at 350ºF.
2) Place the grill pan accessory in the air fryer.
3) In a Ziploc bag, put all ingredients: and give a shake to season all vegetables.
4) Dump all Ingredients: on the grill pan and cook for 20 minutes.
5) Make sure to give the vegetables a shake halfway through the cooking time.

Nutrition information:
Calories:126; Carbs: 17.9g; Protein: 2.9g; Fat: 6.1g

Grilled Sweet Potato Wedges with Dipping Sauce

(Servings: 3, Cooking Time: 20 minutes)

Ingredients:
- 3 medium sweet potatoes, peeled and sliced
- 2 tablespoons olive oil
- Salt and pepper to taste
- ½ cup sour cream
- ½ cup mayonnaise
- 2 tablespoons fresh chives, chopped
- 3 tablespoons Asiago cheese, grated
- 2 tablespoons parmesan cheese

Directions for Cooking:
1) Preheat the air fryer at 350°F.
2) Place the grill pan accessory in the air fryer.
3) Brush the potatoes with olive oil and drizzle with salt and pepper to taste.
4) Place on the grill pan and cook for 20 minutes.
5) Meanwhile, mix the sour cream, mayonnaise, fresh chives, Asiago cheese, and parmesan cheese in a bowl. Season with salt and pepper to taste.
6) Serve the potatoes with the sauce.

Nutrition information:
Calories: 625; Carbs: 50.5g; Protein: 12.7g; Fat: 42.3g

Grilled Green Beans with Shallots

(Servings: 6, Cooking Time: 25 minutes)

Ingredients:
- 1-pound fresh green beans, trimmed
- 2 large shallots, sliced
- 1 tablespoon vegetable oil
- 1 teaspoon soy sauce
- 2 tablespoons fresh basil, chopped
- 1 tablespoon fresh mint, chopped
- 1 tablespoon sesame seeds, toasted
- 2 tablespoons pine nuts

Directions for Cooking:
1) Preheat the air fryer at 350°F.
2) Place the grill pan accessory in the air fryer.
3) In a mixing bowl, combine the green beans, shallots, vegetable oil, and soy sauce.
4) Dump in the air fryer and cook for 25 minutes.
5) Once cooked, garnish with basil, mints, sesame seeds, and pine nuts.

Nutrition information:
Calories:307; Carbs: 11.2g; Protein: 23.7g; Fat: 19.7g

Grille Tomatoes with Garden Herb Salad

(Servings: 4, Cooking Time: 20 minutes)

Ingredients:
- 3 large green tomatoes
- 1 clove of garlic, minced
- 5 tablespoons olive oil
- Salt and pepper to taste
- ¾ cup fresh parsley, chopped
- ¾ cup cilantro leaves, chopped
- ½ cup chopped chives
- 4 leaves iceberg lettuce
- ¼ cup hazelnuts, toasted and chopped
- ¼ cup pistachios, toasted and chopped
- ¼ cup golden raisins
- 2 tablespoons white balsamic vinegar

Directions for Cooking:
1) Preheat the air fryer at 350°F.
2) Place the grill pan accessory in the air fryer.
3) In a mixing bowl, season the tomatoes with garlic, oil, salt and pepper to taste.
4) Place on the grill pan and grill for 20 minutes.
5) Once the tomatoes are done, toss in a salad bowl together with the rest of the ingredients.

Nutrition information:
Calories: 287; Carbs: 12.2g; Protein: 4.8g; Fat: 25.9g

Grilled Potato Packets

(Servings: 3, Cooking Time: 40 minutes)

Ingredients:
- 2 large russet potatoes, peeled and sliced
- 2 medium red sweet potatoes, sliced
- 1 onion, sliced
- 2 tablespoons olive oil
- 1 ½ teaspoons seasoning blend
- Salt and pepper to taste

Directions for Cooking:
1) Preheat the air fryer at 350°F.
2) Place the grill pan accessory in the air fryer.
3) Take a large piece of foil and place all ingredients in the middle. Give a good stir. Fold the foil and crimp the edges.
4) Place the foil on the grill pan.
5) Cook for 40 minutes.

Nutrition information:
Calories: 362; Carbs: 68.4g; Protein: 6.3g; Fat: 9.4g

Sweet Onions

(Servings: 2, Cooking Time: 30 minutes)

Ingredients:
- 2 large sweet onions, sliced
- ½ cup ranch salad dressing
- 2 tablespoons Worcestershire sauce
- 1 teaspoon salad seasoning

Directions for Cooking:
1) Preheat the air fryer at 350°F.
2) Place the grill pan accessory in the air fryer.
3) Place all ingredients in a mixing bowl and give a good stir. Allow the onions to marinate in the fridge for at least 30 minutes.
4) Dump on the grill pan and cook for 30 minutes.

Nutrition information:
Calories: 342; Carbs: 20.8g; Protein: 2.5g; Fat: 4g

Roasted Dill Potato Medley

(Servings: 3, Cooking Time: 30 minutes)

Ingredients:
- 3 Yukon gold potatoes, scrubbed and cut into 1-inch pieces
- 1 ½ cups peeled baby carrots, peeled and sliced
- 1 cup frozen pearl onions, peeled and sliced
- 4 tablespoons olive oil
- 2 tablespoons snipped fresh dill, chopped
- 1 teaspoon salt
- ½ teaspoon black pepper
- 1 lemon, juiced

Directions for Cooking:
1) Preheat the air fryer at 350°F.
2) Place the grill pan accessory in the air fryer.
3) Season the vegetables with the rest of the ingredients.
4) Place on the grill pan and cook for 30 minutes.
5) Be sure to shake the vegetables every 5 minutes to cook evenly.

Nutrition information:
Calories: 480; Carbs: 72.4g; Protein: 8.7g; Fat: 19.1g

Grilled Squash

(Servings: 3, Cooking Time: 20 minutes)

Ingredients:
- 3 zucchinis, cut into quarters
- 1 onion, sliced
- 8 ounces fresh mushrooms, stems removed and sliced
- 1 tablespoon oil
- Salt and pepper to taste
- ½ cup Italian salad dressing

Directions for Cooking:
1) Preheat the air fryer at 350°F.
2) Place the grill pan accessory in the air fryer.
3) Season the zucchini, onion, and mushrooms with oil, salt, and pepper.
4) Place on the grill pan and cook for 20 minutes.
5) Serve with Italian salad dressing.

Nutrition information:
Calories: 367; Carbs: 63.7g; Protein: 8.1 g; Fat: 13.6g

Air Fryer Grilled Fennel

(Servings: 2, Cooking Time: 20 minutes)

Ingredients:
- 2 medium fennel bulbs, peeled and sliced
- 2 tablespoons olive oil
- 3 tablespoons lemon juice
- Salt and pepper to taste
- 4 cloves of garlic, minced

Directions for Cooking:
1) Preheat the air fryer at 350°F.
2) Place the grill pan accessory in the air fryer.
3) Place all ingredients: in a mixing bowl until the fennel slices are well-seasoned.
4) Dump on the grill pan and cook for 20 minutes.

Nutrition information:
Calories: 215; Carbs: 22.7g; Protein: 3.8g; Fat: 14.1g

Grilled Corn Kabobs

(Servings: 2, Cooking Time: 25 minutes)

Ingredients:
- 2 ears of corn
- 2 medium green peppers, cut into large chunks
- 1-pound apricots, halved
- Salt and pepper to taste
- 2 teaspoons prepared mustard

Directions for Cooking:
1) Preheat the air fryer at 350°F.
2) Place the grill pan accessory in the air fryer.
3) On the double layer rack with the skewer accessories, skewer the corn, green peppers, and apricots. Season with salt and pepper to taste.
4) Place skewered corn on the double layer rack and cook for 25 minutes.
5) Once cooked, brush with prepared mustard.

Nutrition information:
Calories: 341; Carbs: 82.5g; Protein: 7.43g; Fat: 2.2g

Grill Smoked Mushrooms

(Servings: 4, Cooking Time: 30 minutes)

Ingredients:
- 4 cups sliced mushrooms
- ¼ cup butter
- 1 teaspoon liquid smoke
- 1 teaspoon poultry seasoning
- Salt and pepper to taste

Directions for Cooking:
1) Preheat the air fryer at 350°F.
2) Place the grill pan accessory in the air fryer.
3) Place all ingredients in a large piece of aluminum foil and mix until well-combined.
4) Close the foil and crimp the edges.
5) Place on the grill pan and cook for 30 minutes.

Nutrition information:
Calories: 109; Carbs:1.5 g; Protein: 0.5g; Fat: 11.6g

Seafood Recipe

Blackened Shrimps in Air Fryer

(Servings: 4, Cooking Time: 6 minutes)

Ingredients:
- 20 jumbo shrimps, peeled and deveined
- 2 tablespoons coconut oil
- 2 teaspoons cilantro
- 2 teaspoons smoked paprika
- 2 teaspoons onion powder
- 1 teaspoon cumin
- 1 teaspoon salt
- 1 teaspoon thyme
- 1 teaspoon oregano
- ¼ teaspoon cayenne pepper
- ¼ teaspoon red chili flakes

Directions for Cooking:
1) Preheat the air fryer at 390ºF.
2) Season the shrimps with all the Ingredients.
3) Place the seasoned shrimps in the double layer rack.
4) Cook for 6 minutes.

Nutrition information:
Calories: 220; Carbs: 2.5g; Protein: 34.2g; Fat: 8.1g

Herb and Garlic Fish Fingers

(Servings: 1, Cooking Time: 10 minutes)

Ingredients:
- ½ pound fish, cut into fingers
- ½ teaspoon salt
- 2 tablespoons lemon juice
- ½ teaspoon turmeric powder
- ½ teaspoon red chili flakes
- 2 teaspoons garlic powder
- ½ teaspoon crushed black pepper
- 1 teaspoon ginger garlic paste
- 2 teaspoons corn flour
- 2 eggs, beaten
- ¼ teaspoon baking soda
- 1 cup bread crumbs
- Oil for brushing

Directions for Cooking:
1) Preheat the air fryer at 390ºF.
2) Season the fish fingers with salt, lemon juice, turmeric powder, chili flakes, garlic powder, black pepper, and garlic paste. Add the corn flour, eggs, and baking soda.
3) Dredge the seasoned fish in breadcrumbs and brush with cooking oil.
4) Place on the double layer rack.
5) Cook for 10 minutes.

Nutrition information:
Calories: 773; Carbs: 32.7g; Protein: 64.9g; Fat: 42.5g

Garlic and Black Pepper Shrimp Grill

(Servings: 2, Cooking Time: 6 minutes)

Ingredients:
- 1 red chili, seeds removed
- 3 cloves of garlic, grated
- 1 tablespoon ground pepper
- 1 tablespoon fresh lime juice
- 1-pound large shrimps, peeled and deveined
- Salt to taste

Directions for Cooking:
1) Preheat the air fryer at 390°F.
2) Place the grill pan accessory in the air fryer.
3) Grill the shrimps for 6 minutes.

Nutrition information:
Calories:179; Carbs: 6.3g; Protein: 31.6g; Fat: 2.3g

Crispy Cod Nuggets with Tartar Sauce

(Servings: 3, Cooking Time: 10 minutes)

Ingredients:
- 1 ½ pounds cod fillet
- Salt and pepper to taste
- ½ cup flour
- 1 egg, beaten
- 1 cup cracker crumbs
- 1 tablespoon vegetable oil
- ½ cup non-fat mayonnaise
- 1 teaspoon honey
- Zest from half of a lemon
- Juice from half a lemon
- ½ teaspoon Worcestershire sauce
- 1 tablespoon sweet pickle relish
- Salt and pepper to taste

Directions for Cooking:
1) Preheat the air fryer at 390°F.
2) Season the cods with salt and pepper.
3) Dredge the fish on flour and dip in the beaten egg before dredging on the cracker crumbs. Brush with oil.
4) Place the fish on the double layer rack and cook for 10 minutes.
5) Meanwhile, prepare the sauce by mixing all ingredients in a bowl.
6) Serve the fish with the sauce.

Nutrition information:
Calories: 470; Carbs: 25.4g; Protein: 42.9g; Fat: 21.8g

Grilled Salmon with Cucumbers

(Servings: 4, Cooking Time: 10 minutes)

Ingredients:
- 4 6-ounces salmon fillets
- 1 teaspoon lemon zest
- Juice from 1 lemon, freshly squeezed
- 1 tablespoon fresh dill
- Salt and pepper to taste
- ½ cup mayonnaise
- ½ cup sour cream
- 2 cucumbers peeled and sliced

Directions for Cooking:
1) Preheat the air fryer at 390°F.
2) Place the grill pan accessory in the air fryer.
3) Season the salmon fillets with lemon zest, lemon juice, dill, salt and pepper.
4) Grill the salmon for 10 minutes making sure to flip halfway through the cooking time.
5) Meanwhile, prepare the cucumber salad by mixing in a bowl the mayonnaise, sour cream and cucumber slices. Season with salt and pepper.
6) Serve the salmon with the cucumber salad.

Nutrition information:
Calories: 409; Carbs: 5.9g; Protein: 38.4g; Fat: 25.1g

Shrimps, Zucchini, And Tomatoes on the Grill

(Servings: 2, Cooking Time: 15 minutes)

Ingredients:
- 10 jumbo shrimps, peeled and deveined
- Salt and pepper to taste
- 1 clove of garlic, minced
- 1 medium zucchini, sliced
- 1-pint cherry tomatoes
- ¼ cup feta cheese

Directions for Cooking:
1) Preheat the air fryer at 390°F.
2) Place the grill pan accessory in the air fryer.
3) In a mixing bowl, season the shrimps with salt and pepper. Stir in the garlic, zucchini, and tomatoes.
4) Place on the grill pan and cook for 15 minutes.
5) Once cooked, transfer to a bowl and sprinkle with feta cheese.

Nutrition information:
Calories: 257; Carbs: 4.2 g; Protein: 48.9g; Fat: 5.3g

Grilled Halibut with Tomatoes and Hearts of Palm

(Servings: 4, Cooking Time: 15 minutes)

Ingredients:
- 4 halibut fillets
- Juice from 1 lemon
- Salt and pepper to taste
- 2 tablespoons oil
- ½ cup hearts of palm, rinse and drained
- 1 cup cherry tomatoes

Directions for Cooking:
1) Preheat the air fryer at 390°F.
2) Place the grill pan accessory in the air fryer.
3) Season the halibut fillets with lemon juice, salt and pepper. Brush with oil.
4) Place the fish on the grill pan.
5) Arrange the hearts of palms and cherry tomatoes on the side and sprinkle with more salt and pepper.
6) Cook for 15 minutes.

Nutrition information:
Calories: 208; Carbs: 7g; Protein: 21 g; Fat: 11g

Chat Masala Grilled Snapper

(Servings: 5, Cooking Time: 25 minutes)

Ingredients:
- 2 ½ pounds whole fish
- Salt to taste
- 1/3 cup chat masala
- 3 tablespoons fresh lime juice
- 5 tablespoons olive oil

Directions for Cooking:
1) Preheat the air fryer at 390°F.
2) Place the grill pan accessory in the air fryer.
3) Season the fish with salt, chat masala and lime juice.
4) Brush with oil
5) Place the fish on a foil basket and place inside the grill.
6) Cook for 25 minutes.

Nutrition information:
Calories:308 ; Carbs: 0.7g; Protein: 35.2g; Fat: 17.4g

One-Pan Shrimp and Chorizo Mix Grill

(Servings: 4, Cooking Time: 15 minutes)

Ingredients:
- 1 ½ pounds large shrimps, peeled and deveined
- Salt and pepper to taste
- 6 links fresh chorizo sausage
- 2 bunches asparagus spears, trimmed
- Lime wedges

Directions for Cooking:
1) Preheat the air fryer at 390°F.
2) Place the grill pan accessory in the air fryer.
3) Season the shrimps with salt and pepper to taste. Set aside.
4) Place the chorizo on the grill pan and the sausage.
5) Place the asparagus on top.
6) Grill for 15 minutes.
7) Serve with lime wedges.

Nutrition information:
Calories:124 ; Carbs: 9.4g; Protein: 8.2g; Fat: 7.1g

Grilled Tasty Scallops

(Servings: 2, Cooking Time: 10 minutes)

Ingredients:
- 1-pound sea scallops, cleaned and patted dry
- Salt and pepper to taste
- 3 dried chilies
- 2 tablespoon dried thyme
- 1 tablespoon dried oregano
- 1 tablespoon ground coriander
- 1 tablespoon ground fennel
- 2 teaspoons chipotle pepper

Directions for Cooking:
1) Preheat the air fryer at 390°F.
2) Place the grill pan accessory in the air fryer.
3) Mix all Ingredients: in a bowl.
4) Dump the scallops on the grill pan and cook for 10 minutes.

Nutrition information:
Calories:291 ; Carbs: 20.7g; Protein: 48.6g; Fat: 2.5g

Clam with Lemons on the Grill

(Servings: 6, Cooking Time: 6 minutes)

Ingredients:
- 4 pounds littleneck clams
- Salt and pepper to taste
- 1 clove of garlic, minced
- ½ cup parsley, chopped
- 1 teaspoon crushed red pepper flakes
- 5 tablespoons olive oil
- 1 loaf crusty bread, halved
- ½ cup parmesan cheese, grated

Directions for Cooking:
1) Preheat the air fryer at 390°F.
2) Place the grill pan accessory in the air fryer.
3) Place the clams on the grill pan and cook for 6 minutes.
4) Once the clams have opened, take them out and extract the meat.
5) Transfer the meat into a bowl and season with salt and pepper.
6) Stir in the garlic, parsley, red pepper flakes, and olive oil.
7) Serve on top of bread and sprinkle with parmesan cheese.

Nutrition information:
Calories: 341; Carbs: 26g; Protein: 48.3g; Fat: 17.2g

Salmon Steak Grilled with Cilantro Garlic Sauce

(Servings: 2, Cooking Time: 15 minutes)

Ingredients:
- 2 salmon steaks
- Salt and pepper to taste
- 2 tablespoons vegetable oil
- 2 cloves of garlic, minced
- 1 cup cilantro leaves
- ½ cup Greek yogurt
- 1 teaspoon honey

Directions for Cooking:
1) Preheat the air fryer at 390°F.
2) Place the grill pan accessory in the air fryer.
3) Season the salmon steaks with salt and pepper. Brush with oil.
4) Grill for 15 minutes and make sure to flip halfway through the cooking time.
5) In a food processor, mix the garlic, cilantro leaves, yogurt and honey. Season with salt and pepper to taste. Pulse until smooth.
6) Serve the salmon steaks with the cilantro sauce.

Nutrition information:
Calories: 485; Carbs: 6.3g; Protein: 47.6g; Fat: 29.9g

Tasty Grilled Red Mullet

(Servings: 8, Cooking Time: 15 minutes)

Ingredients:
- 8 whole red mullets, gutted and scales removed
- Salt and pepper to taste
- Juice from 1 lemon
- 1 tablespoon olive oil

Directions for Cooking:
1) Preheat the air fryer at 390°F.
2) Place the grill pan accessory in the air fryer.
3) Season the red mullet with salt, pepper, and lemon juice.
4) Brush with olive oil.
5) Grill for 15 minutes.

Nutrition information:
Calories: 152; Carbs: 0.9g; Protein: 23.1g; Fat: 6.2g

Chargrilled Halibut Niçoise With Vegetables

(Servings: 6, Cooking Time: 15 minutes)

Ingredients:
- 1 ½ pounds halibut fillets
- Salt and pepper to taste
- 2 tablespoons olive oil
- 2 pounds mixed vegetables
- 4 cups torn lettuce leaves
- 1 cup cherry tomatoes, halved
- 4 large hard-boiled eggs, peeled and sliced

Directions for Cooking:
1) Preheat the air fryer at 390°F.
2) Place the grill pan accessory in the air fryer.
3) Rub the halibut with salt and pepper. Brush the fish with oil.
4) Place on the grill.
5) Surround the fish fillet with the mixed vegetables and cook for 15 minutes.
6) Assemble the salad by serving the fish fillet with grilled mixed vegetables, lettuce, cherry tomatoes, and hard-boiled eggs.

Nutrition information:
Calories: 312; Carbs: 16.8 g; Protein: 19.8g; Fat: 18.3g

Spiced Salmon Kebabs

(Servings: 3, Cooking Time: 15 minutes)

Ingredients:
- 2 tablespoons chopped fresh oregano
- 2 teaspoons sesame seeds
- 1 teaspoon ground cumin
- Salt and pepper to taste
- 1 ½ pounds salmon fillets
- 2 tablespoons olive oil
- 2 lemons, sliced into rounds

Directions for Cooking:
1) Preheat the air fryer at 390°F.
2) Place the grill pan accessory in the air fryer.
3) Create the dry rub by combining the oregano, sesame seeds, cumin, salt and pepper.
4) Rub the salmon fillets with the dry rub and brush with oil.
5) Grill the salmon for 15 minutes.
6) Serve with lemon slices once cooked.

Nutrition information:
Calories per serving 447 ; Carbs: 4.1g; Protein:47.6 g; Fat:26.6 g

Roasted Tuna on Linguine

(Servings: 2, Cooking Time: 20 minutes)

Ingredients:
- 1-pound fresh tuna fillets
- Salt and pepper to taste
- 1 tablespoon olive oil
- 12 ounces linguine, cooked according to package Directions for Cooking:
- 2 cups parsley leaves, chopped
- 1 tablespoon capers, chopped
- Juice from 1 lemon

Directions for Cooking:
1) Preheat the air fryer at 390°F.
2) Place the grill pan accessory in the air fryer.
3) Season the tuna with salt and pepper. Brush with oil.
4) Grill for 20 minutes.
5) Once the tuna is cooked, shred using forks and place on top of cooked linguine. Add parsley and capers. Season with salt and pepper and add lemon juice.

Nutrition information:
Calories: 520; Carbs: 60.6g; Protein: 47.7g; Fat: 9.6g

Chili Lime Clams with Tomatoes

(Servings: 3, Cooking Time: 15 minutes)

Ingredients:
- 25 littleneck clams
- 1 tablespoon fresh lime juice
- Salt and pepper to taste
- 6 tablespoons unsalted butter
- 4 cloves of garlic, minced
- ½ cup tomatoes, chopped
- ½ cup basil leaves

Directions for Cooking:
1) Preheat the air fryer at 390°F.
2) Place the grill pan accessory in the air fryer.
3) On a large foil, place all ingredients. Fold over the foil and close by crimping the edges.
4) Place on the grill pan and cook for 15 minutes.
5) Serve with bread.

Nutrition information:
Calories: 163; Carbs: 4.1g; Protein: 1.7g; Fat: 15.5g

Air Fryer Garlicky-Grilled Turbot

(Servings: 2, Cooking Time: 20 minutes)

Ingredients:
- 2 whole turbot, scaled and head removed
- Salt and pepper to taste
- 1 clove of garlic, minced
- ½ cup chopped celery leaves
- 2 tablespoons olive oil

Directions for Cooking:
1) Preheat the air fryer at 390°F.
2) Place the grill pan accessory in the air fryer.
3) Season the turbot with salt, pepper, garlic, and celery leaves.
4) Brush with oil.
5) Place on the grill pan and cook for 20 minutes until the fish becomes flaky.

Nutrition information:
Calories: 269; Carbs: 3.3g; Protein: 66.2g; Fat: 25.6g

Broiled Spiced-Lemon Squid

(Servings: 4, Cooking Time: 15 minutes)

Ingredients:
- 2 pounds squid, gutted and cleaned
- Salt and pepper to taste
- 1 tablespoon fresh lemon juice
- 5 cloves of garlic
- ½ cup tomatoes, chopped
- ½ cup green onions, chopped
- 2 tablespoons olive oil

Directions for Cooking:
1) Preheat the air fryer at 390°F.
2) Place the grill pan accessory in the air fryer.
3) Season the squid with salt, pepper, and lemon juice.
4) Stuff the cavity with garlic, tomatoes, and onions.
5) Brush the squid with olive oil.
6) Place on the grill pan and cook for 15 minutes.
7) Halfway through the cooking time, flip the squid.

Nutrition information:
Calories: 277; Carbs: 10.7g; Protein: 36g; Fat: 10g

Tuna Grill with Ginger Sauce

(Servings: 3, Cooking Time: 20 minutes)

Ingredients:
- 1 ½ pounds tuna, thick slices
- 2 tablespoons rice vinegar
- 2 tablespoons grated fresh ginger
- 2 tablespoons peanut oil
- 2 tablespoons soy sauce
- 2 tablespoons honey
- 1 serrano chili, seeded and minced

Directions for Cooking:
1) Place all ingredients in a Ziploc bag.
2) Allow to marinate in the fridge for at least 2 hours.
3) Preheat the air fryer at 390°F.
4) Place the grill pan accessory in the air fryer.
5) Grill the fish for 15 to 20 minutes.
6) Flip the fish halfway through the cooking time.
7) Meanwhile, pour the marinade in a saucepan and allow to simmer for 10 minutes until the sauce thickens.
8) Brush the tuna with the sauce before serving.

Nutrition information:
Calories: 357; Carbs:14.8 g; Protein: 44.9g; Fat: 13.1g

Char-Grilled Spicy Halibut

(Servings: 6, Cooking Time: 20 minutes)

Ingredients:
- 3 pounds halibut fillet, skin removed
- Salt and pepper to taste
- 4 tablespoons dry white wine
- 4 tablespoons olive oil
- 2 cloves of garlic, minced
- 1 tablespoon chili powder

Directions for Cooking:
1) Place all ingredients in a Ziploc bag.
2) Allow to marinate in the fridge for at least 2 hours.
3) Preheat the air fryer at 390°F.
4) Place the grill pan accessory in the air fryer.
5) Grill the fish for 20 minutes making sure to flip every 5 minutes.

Nutrition information:
Calories: 385; Carbs: 1.7g; Protein: 33g; Fat: 40.6g

Roasted Swordfish with Charred Leeks

(Servings: 4, Cooking Time: 20 minutes)

Ingredients:
- 4 swordfish steaks
- Salt and pepper to taste
- 3 tablespoons lime juice
- 2 tablespoons olive oil
- 4 medium leeks, cut into an inch long

Directions for Cooking:
1) Preheat the air fryer at 390°F.
2) Place the grill pan accessory in the air fryer.
3) Season the swordfish with salt, pepper and lime juice.
4) Brush the fish with olive oil
5) Place fish fillets on grill pan and top with leeks.
6) Grill for 20 minutes.

Nutrition information:
Calories: 611; Carbs: 14.6g; Protein: 48g; Fat: 40g

Citrusy Branzini on the Grill

(Servings: 2, Cooking Time: 15 minutes)

Ingredients:
- 2 branzini fillets
- Salt and pepper to taste
- 3 lemons, juice freshly squeezed
- 2 oranges, juice freshly squeezed

Directions for Cooking:
1) Place all ingredients in a Ziploc bag. Allow to marinate in the fridge for 2 hours.
2) Preheat the air fryer at 390°F.
3) Place the grill pan accessory in the air fryer.
4) Place the fish on the grill pan and cook for 15 minutes until the fish is flaky.

Nutrition information:
Calories: 318; Carbs: 20.8g; Protein: 23.5g; Fat: 15.6g

Grilled Squid Rings with Kale and Tomatoes

(Servings: 3, Cooking Time: 15 minutes)

Ingredients:
- 1 2-pound squid, cleaned and sliced into rings
- Salt and pepper to taste
- 3 cloves of garlic, minced
- 1 sprig rosemary, chopped
- ¼ cup red wine vinegar
- 3 pounds kale, torn
- 3 tomatoes, chopped

Directions for Cooking:
1) Preheat the air fryer at 390°F.
2) Place the grill pan accessory in the air fryer.
3) Season the squid rings with salt, pepper, garlic, rosemary, and wine vinegar.
4) Grill for 15 minutes.
5) Serve octopus on a bed of kale leaves and garnish with tomatoes on top.

Nutrition information:
Calories: 575; Carbs: 56.2g; Protein: 68.1g; Fat: 8.6g

Grilled Shrimp with Butter

(Servings: 4, Cooking Time: 15 minutes)

Ingredients:
- 6 tablespoons unsalted butter
- ½ cup red onion, chopped
- 1 ½ teaspoon red pepper
- 1 teaspoon shrimp paste or fish sauce
- 1 ½ teaspoon lime juice
- Salt and pepper to taste
- 24 large shrimps, shelled and deveined

Directions for Cooking:
1) Preheat the air fryer at 390°F.
2) Place the grill pan accessory in the air fryer.
3) Place all ingredients in a Ziploc bag and give a good shake.
4) Skewer the shrimps through a bamboo skewer and place on the grill pan.
5) Cook for 15 minutes.
6) Flip the shrimps halfway through the cooking time.

Nutrition information:
Calories: 153; Carbs: 2.3g; Protein: 6.9g; Fat: 12.9g

Char-Grilled 'n Herbed Sea Scallops

(Servings: 3, Cooking Time: 10 minutes)

Ingredients:
- 1-pound sea scallops, meat only
- 3 tablespoons olive oil, divided
- 1 teaspoon dried sage
- Salt and pepper to taste
- 1 cup grape tomatoes, halved
- 1/3 cup basil leaves, shredded

Directions for Cooking:
1) Preheat the air fryer at 390°F.
2) Place the grill pan accessory in the air fryer.
3) Season the scallops with half of the olive oil, sage, salt and pepper.
4) Toss into the air fryer and grill for 10 minutes.
5) Once cooked, serve with tomatoes and basil leaves.
6) Drizzle the remaining olive oil and season with more salt and pepper to taste.

Nutrition information:
Calories: 336; Carbs: 18g; Protein: 32g; Fat: 15g

Japanese Citrus Soy Squid

(Servings: 4, Cooking Time: 10 minutes)

Ingredients:
- ½ cup mirin
- 1 cup soy sauce
- 1/3 cup yuzu or orange juice, freshly squeezed
- 2 cups water
- 2 pounds squid body, cut into rings

Directions for Cooking:
1) Place all ingredients in a Ziploc bag and allow the squid rings to marinate in the fridge for at least 2 hours.
2) Preheat the air fryer at 390°F.
3) Place the grill pan accessory in the air fryer.
4) Grill the squid rings for 10 minutes.
5) Meanwhile, pour the marinade over a sauce pan and allow to simmer for 10 minutes or until the sauce has reduced.
6) Baste the squid rings with the sauce before serving.

Nutrition information:
Calories: 412; Carbs: 4.1g; Protein: 44.2g; Fat: 24.3g

Greek-Style Grilled Scallops

(Servings: 3, Cooking Time: 15 minutes)

Ingredients:
- ¼ cup Greek yogurt
- A pinch of saffron threads
- 1 ½ teaspoons rice vinegar
- Salt and pepper to taste
- 12 large sea scallops
- 2 tablespoons olive oil

Directions for Cooking:
1) Place all ingredients in a Ziploc bag and allow the scallops to marinate in the fridge for at least 2 hours.
2) Preheat the air fryer at 390°F.
3) Place the grill pan accessory in the air fryer.
4) Grill the scallops for 15 minutes.
5) Serve on bread and drizzle with more olive oil if desired.

Nutrition information:
Calories: 178; Carbs: 6g; Protein: 16g; Fat: 10g

Easy Grilled Pesto Scallops

(Servings: 3, Cooking Time: 15 minutes)

Ingredients:
- 12 large scallops, side muscles removed
- Salt and pepper to taste
- ½ cup prepared commercial pesto

Directions for Cooking:
1) Place all ingredients in a Ziploc bag and allow the scallops to marinate in the fridge for at least 2 hours.
2) Preheat the air fryer at 390°F.
3) Place the grill pan accessory in the air fryer.
4) Grill the scallops for 15 minutes.
5) Serve on pasta or bread if desired.

Nutrition information:
Calories: 137; Carbs: 7.7g; Protein: 15.3 g; Fat: 5g

Clams with Herbed Butter in Packets

(Servings: 2, Cooking Time: 20 minutes)

Ingredients:
- 24 littleneck clams, scrubbed clean
- ½ cup unsalted butter, diced
- Salt and pepper to taste
- 1 tablespoon fresh lemon juice
- 1 tablespoon parsley, chopped
- 1 tablespoon dill, chopped
- Lemon wedges

Directions for Cooking:
1) Preheat the air fryer at 390°F.
2) Place the grill pan accessory in the air fryer.
3) On a large foil, place the clams and the rest of the ingredients.
4) Fold the foil and crimp the edges.
5) Place on the grill pan and cook for 15 to 20 minutes or until all clams have opened.

Nutrition information:
Calories: 384; Carbs: 6g; Protein: 18g; Fat: 32g

Simple Sesame Squid on the Grill

(Servings: 3, Cooking Time: 10 minutes)

Ingredients:
- 1 ½ pounds squid, cleaned
- 2 tablespoon toasted sesame oil
- Salt and pepper to taste

Directions for Cooking:
1) Preheat the air fryer at 390°F.
2) Place the grill pan accessory in the air fryer.
3) Season the squid with sesame oil, salt and pepper.
4) Grill the squid for 10 minutes.

Nutrition information:
Calories: 220; Carbs: 0.9g; Protein: 27g; Fat: 12g

Grilled Shellfish with Vegetables

(Servings: 8, Cooking Time: 30 minutes)

Ingredients:
- 1 bunch broccolini
- 8 asparagus spears
- 8 small carrots, peeled and sliced
- 4 tomatoes, halved
- 1 red onion, wedged
- 2 tablespoons olive oil
- Salt and pepper to taste
- 16 small oysters, scrubbed
- 16 littleneck clams, scrubbed
- 24 large mussels, scrubbed
- 2 tablespoons lemon juice
- 4 basil sprigs

Directions for Cooking:
1) Preheat the air fryer at 390°F.
2) Place the grill pan accessory in the air fryer.
3) Place all vegetables in a bowl and drizzle with oil. Season with salt and pepper then toss to coat the vegetables with the seasoning.
4) Place on the grill pan and grill for 15 minutes or until the edges of the vegetables are charred. Set aside
5) On a large foil, place all the shellfish and season with salt, lemon juice, and basil. Fold the foil and crimp the edges.
6) Place the foil packet on the grill pan and cook for another 15 minutes or until the shellfish have opened.
7) Serve the shellfish with the charred vegetables.

Nutrition information:
Calories: 282; Carbs: 20g; Protein: 26.7g; Fat: 10.5g

Grilled Meat Recipes

Skirt Steak with Mojo Marinade

(Servings: 4, Cooking Time: 60 minutes)

Ingredients:
- 2 pounds skirt steak, trimmed from excess fat
- 2 tablespoons lime juice
- ¼ cup orange juice
- 2 tablespoons olive oil
- 4 cloves of garlic, minced
- 1 teaspoon ground cumin
- Salt and pepper to taste

Directions for Cooking:
1) Place all ingredients in a mixing bowl and allow to marinate in the fridge for at least 2 hours
2) Preheat the air fryer at 390°F.
3) Place the grill pan accessory in the air fryer.
4) Grill for 15 minutes per batch and flip the beef every 8 minutes for even grilling.
5) Meanwhile, pour the marinade on a saucepan and allow to simmer for 10 minutes or until the sauce thickens.
6) Slice the beef and pour over the sauce.

Nutrition information:
Calories: 568; Carbs: 4.7g; Protein: 59.1g; Fat: 34.7g

Dijon-Marinated Skirt Steak

(Servings: 2, Cooking Time: 40 minutes)

Ingredients:
- ¼ cup Dijon mustard
- 1-pound skirt steak, trimmed
- 2 tablespoons champagne vinegar
- 1 tablespoon rosemary leaves
- Salt and pepper to taste

Directions for Cooking:
1) Place all ingredients in a Ziploc bag and marinate in the fridge for 2 hours.
2) Preheat the air fryer at 390°F.
3) Place the grill pan accessory in the air fryer.
4) Grill the skirt steak for 20 minutes per batch.
5) Flip the beef halfway through the cooking time.

Nutrition information:
Calories: 516; Carbs: 4.2g; Protein: 60.9g; Fat: 28.4g

Grilled Carne Asada Steak

(Servings: 2, Cooking Time: 50 minutes)

Ingredients:
- 2 slices skirt steak
- 1 dried ancho chilies, chopped
- 1 chipotle pepper, chopped
- 2 tablespoons of fresh lemon juice
- 2 tablespoons olive oil
- 3 cloves of garlic, minced
- 1 tablespoons soy sauce
- 2 tablespoons Asian fish sauce
- 1 tablespoon cumin
- 1 tablespoon coriander seeds
- 2 tablespoons brown sugar

Directions for Cooking:
1) Place all ingredients in a Ziploc bag and marinate in the fridge for 2 hours.
2) Preheat the air fryer at 390°F.
3) Place the grill pan accessory in the air fryer.
4) Grill the skirt steak for 20 minutes.
5) Flip the steak every 10 minutes for even grilling.

Nutrition information:
Calories: 697; Carbs: 10.2g; Protein: 62.7 g; Fat: 45g

Chimichurri-Style Steak

(Servings: 6, Cooking Time: 60 minutes)

Ingredients:
- 3 pounds steak
- Salt and pepper to taste
- 1 cup commercial chimichurri

Directions for Cooking:
1) Place all ingredients in a Ziploc bag and marinate in the fridge for 2 hours.
2) Preheat the air fryer at 390°F.
3) Place the grill pan accessory in the air fryer.
4) Grill the skirt steak for 20 minutes per batch.
5) Flip the steak every 10 minutes for even grilling.

Nutrition information:
Calories: 507; Carbs: 2.8g; Protein: 63g; Fat: 27g

Strip Steak with Cucumber Yogurt Sauce

(Servings: 2, Cooking Time: 50 minutes)

Ingredients:
- 2 New York strip steaks
- Salt and pepper to taste
- 3 tablespoons olive oil
- 1 cucumber, seeded and chopped
- 1 cup Greek yogurt
- ½ cup parsley, chopped

Directions for Cooking:
1) Preheat the air fryer at 390°F.
2) Place the grill pan accessory in the air fryer.
3) Season the strip steaks with salt and pepper. Drizzle with oil.
4) Grill the steak for 20 minutes per batch and make sure to flip the meat every 10 minutes for even grilling.
5) Meanwhile, combine the cucumber, yogurt, and parsley.
6) Serve the beef with the cucumber yogurt.

Nutrition information:
Calories: 460; Carbs: 5.2g; Protein: 50.8g; Fat: 26.3g

Grilled BBQ Sausages

(Servings: 3, Cooking Time: 30 minutes)

Ingredients:
- 6 sausage links
- ½ cup prepared BBQ sauce

for Cooking:
1) Preheat the air fryer at 390°F.
2) Place the grill pan accessory in the air fryer.
3) Place the sausage links and grill for 30 minutes.
4) Flip halfway through the cooking time.
5) Before serving brush with prepared BBQ sauce.

Nutrition information:
Calories: 265; Carbs: 6.4g; Protein: 27.7g; Fat: 14.2g

Medium Rare Simple Salt and Pepper Steak

(Servings: 3, Cooking Time: 30 minutes)

Ingredients:
- 1 ½ pounds skirt steak
- Salt and pepper to taste

Directions for Cooking:
1) Preheat the air fryer at 390°F.
2) Place the grill pan accessory in the air fryer.
3) Season the skirt steak with salt and pepper.
4) Place on the grill pan and cook for 15 minutes per batch.
5) Flip the meat halfway through the cooking time.

Nutrition information:
Calories: 469; Carbs: 1g; Protein: 60g; Fat: 25g

Pounded Flank Steak with Tomato Salsa

(Servings: 4, Cooking Time: 40 minutes)

Ingredients:
- 1 ½ pounds flank steak, pounded
- Salt and pepper to taste
- 2 cups chopped tomatoes
- ¼ cup chopped cilantro
- 1 red onion, chopped
- 1 teaspoon coriander powder

Directions for Cooking:
1) Preheat the air fryer at 390°F.
2) Place the grill pan accessory in the air fryer.
3) Season the flank steak with salt and pepper.
4) Grill for 20 minutes per batch and make sure to flip the beef halfway through the cooking time.
5) Meanwhile, prepare the salsa by mixing in a bowl the tomatoes, cilantro, onions, and coriander. Season with more salt and pepper to taste.

Nutrition information:
Calories: 243; Carbs: 4g; Protein: 37.4g; Fat: 8.6g

Strip Steak with Japanese Dipping Sauce

(Servings: 2, Cooking Time: 40 minutes)

Ingredients:
- 2 strip steaks
- Salt and pepper to taste
- 1 tablespoon olive oil
- ½ cup soy sauce
- ½ cup rice wine vinegar
- ¼ cup grated daikon radish

Directions for Cooking:
1) Preheat the air fryer at 390°F.
2) Place the grill pan accessory in the air fryer.
3) Season the steak with salt and pepper.
4) Brush with oil.
5) Grill for 20 minutes per piece and make sure to flip the beef halfway through the cooking time
6) Prepare the dipping sauce by combining the soy sauce and vinegar.
7) Serve the steak with the sauce and daikon radish.

Nutrition information:
Calories: 510; Carbs:19.3 g; Protein: 54g; Fat: 24g

Chi Spacca's Bistecca

(Servings: 4, Cooking Time: 45 minutes)

Ingredients:
- 2 pounds bone-in rib eye steak
- Salt and pepper to taste
- 1 packet Italian herb mix
- 1 tablespoon olive oil

Directions for Cooking:
1) Preheat the air fryer at 390°F.
2) Place the grill pan accessory in the air fryer.
3) Season the steak with salt, pepper, Italian herb mix, and olive oil. Cover top with foil.
4) Grill for 45 minutes and flip the steak halfway through the cooking time.

Nutrition information:
Calories: 481; Carbs:1.1 g; Protein: 50.9g; Fat: 30.3g

Grilled Steak with Parsley Salad

(Servings: 4, Cooking Time: 45 minutes)

Ingredients:
- 1 ½ pounds flatiron steak
- 3 tablespoons olive oil
- Salt and pepper to taste
- 2 cups parsley leaves
- ½ cup parmesan cheese, grated
- 1 tablespoon fresh lemon juice

Directions for Cooking:
1) Preheat the air fryer at 390°F.
2) Place the grill pan accessory in the air fryer.
3) Mix together the steak, oil, salt and pepper.
4) Grill for 15 minutes per batch and make sure to flip the meat halfway through the cooking time.
5) Meanwhile, prepare the salad by combining in a bowl the parsley leaves, parmesan cheese and lemon juice. Season with salt and pepper.

Nutrition information:
Calories: 595; Carbs: 4.9g; Protein: 47g; Fat: 43g

Korean Grilled Skirt Steak

(Servings: 1, Cooking Time: 30 minutes)

Ingredients:
- 3 tablespoons gochujang sauce
- 3 tablespoons olive oil
- 3 tablespoons rice vinegar
- Salt and pepper to taste
- 1 skirt steak, halved

Directions for Cooking:
1) Preheat the air fryer at 390°F.
2) Place the grill pan accessory in the air fryer.
3) Rub all spices and seasonings on the skirt steak.
4) Place on the grill and cook for 15 minutes per batch.
5) Flip the steak halfway through the cooking time.
6) Serve with more gochujang or kimchi.

Nutrition information:
Calories: 467; Carbs: 8.3g; Protein:9.3 g; Fat: 44g

Onion Marinated Skirt Steak

(Servings: 3, Cooking Time: 45 minutes)

Ingredients:
- 1 large red onion, grated or pureed
- 2 tablespoons brown sugar
- 1 tablespoon vinegar
- 1 ½ pounds skirt steak
- Salt and pepper to taste

Directions for Cooking:
1) Place all ingredients in a Ziploc bag and allow to marinate in the fridge for at least 2 hours.
2) Preheat the air fryer at 390°F.
3) Place the grill pan accessory in the air fryer.
4) Grill for 15 minutes per batch.
5) Flip every 8 minutes for even grilling.

Nutrition information:
Calories: 512; Carbs: 6g; Protein: 60.1g; Fat: 27.5g

Grilled Beef Steak with Herby Marinade

(Servings: 2, Cooking Time: 40 minutes)

Ingredients:
- 2 porterhouse steaks
- Salt and pepper to taste
- ¼ cup fish sauce
- 2 tablespoons marjoram
- 2 tablespoons thyme
- 2 tablespoons sage

Directions for Cooking:
1) Place all ingredients in a Ziploc bag and allow to marinate in the fridge for at least 2 hours.
2) Preheat the air fryer at 390°F.
3) Place the grill pan accessory in the air fryer.
4) Grill for 20 minutes per batch.
5) Flip every 10 minutes for even grilling.

Nutrition information:
Calories: 1189; Carbs: 6.3g; Protein: 112.5g; Fat: 79.3g

Dessert & Snacks Recipes

Crunchy Crisped Peaches

(Servings: 4, Cooking Time: 30 minutes)

Ingredients:
- 4 cup sliced peaches, frozen
- 3 tablespoon sugar
- 2 tablespoon Flour, white
- 1 teaspoon sugar, white
- 1/4 cup Flour, white
- 1/3 cup oats, dry rolled
- 3 tablespoon butter, unsalted
- 1 teaspoon cinnamon
- 3 tablespoon pecans, chopped

Directions for Cooking:

1) Lightly grease baking pan of air fryer with cooking spray. Mix in a tsp cinnamon, 2 tbsp flour, 3 tbsp sugar, and peaches.
2) For 20 minutes, cook on 300°F.
3) Mix the rest of the Ingredients: in a bowl. Pour over peaches.
4) Cook for 10 minutes at 330°F.
5) Serve and enjoy.

Nutrition Information:
Calories: 435; Carbs: 74.1g; Protein: 4.3g; Fat: 13.4g

Sour Cream-Blueberry Coffee Cake

(Servings: 6, Cooking Time: 35 minutes)

Ingredients:
- 1/2 cup butter, softened
- 1 cup white sugar
- 1 egg
- 1/2 cup sour cream
- 1/2 teaspoon vanilla extract
- 3/4 cup and 1 tablespoon all-purpose flour
- 1/2 teaspoon baking powder
- 1/8 teaspoon salt
- 1/2 cup fresh or frozen blueberries
- 1/4 cup brown sugar
- 1/2 teaspoon ground cinnamon
- 1/4 cup chopped pecans
- 1-1/2 teaspoons confectioners' sugar for dusting

Directions for Cooking:

1) In a small bowl, whisk well pecans, cinnamon, and brown sugar.
2) In a blender, blend well all wet Ingredients. Add dry Ingredients: except for confectioner's sugar and blueberries. Blend well until smooth and creamy.
3) Lightly grease baking pan of air fryer with cooking spray.
4) Pour half of batter in pan. Sprinkle half of pecan mixture on top. Pour the remaining batter. And then topped with remaining pecan mixture.
5) Cover pan with foil.
6) For 35 minutes, cook on 330°F.
7) Serve and enjoy with a dusting of confectioner's sugar.

Nutrition Information:
Calories: 471; Carbs: 59.5g; Protein: 4.1g; Fat: 24.0g

Five-Cheese Pull Apart Bread

(Servings: 2, Cooking Time: 15 minutes)

Ingredients:
- 1 Large Bread Loaf
- 100 g Butter
- 2 Tsp Garlic Puree
- 30 g Cheddar Cheese
- 30 g Goats Cheese
- 30 g Mozzarella Cheese
- 30 g Soft Cheese
- 30 g Edam Cheese
- 2 Tsp Chives
- Salt & Pepper

Directions for Cooking:
1) Grate hard cheese and separate into 4 piles.
2) Lightly grease baking pan of air fryer with cooking spray. Melt butter for 2 minutes at 330ºF. Stir in garlic, pepper, salt, and chives and cook for 3 minutes.
3) Make slits on bread and pour melted butter into slits. Cover with soft cheese all the slits. Followed by remaining cheeses. Insert in all the slits on the bread.
4) Place bread in air fryer basket.
5) Cook for 10 minutes at 330ºF.
6) Serve and enjoy.

Nutrition Information:
Calories: 518; Carbs: 13.3g; Protein: 21.4g; Fat: 42.1g

Buttery Dinner Rolls

(Servings: 9, Cooking Time: 25 minutes)

Ingredients:
- 1 cup Fresh Milk (room temperature)
- 114gn Butter (softened) and more for brushing
- 63gm Sugar
- 2 Eggs
- 1 1/2 tsp Salt
- 508gm Bread Flour
- 2 1/4 tsp Instant Yeast

Directions for Cooking:
1) In mixer, mix all wet Ingredients. Followed by dry Ingredients: and knead for at least 10 minutes. Roll dough into 9 rolls.
2) Lightly grease baking pan of air fryer with cooking spray. Place rolls in a single layer. Cover top of pan with damp cloth and rolls rise for at least an hour.
3) For 15 minutes, cook on 330ºF. Halfway through cooking time, stir.
4) Add butter slices on top of rolls.
5) Serve and enjoy.

Nutrition Information:
Calories: 300; Carbs: 31.2g; Protein: 7.7g; Fat: 16.0g

Yummy Carrot Cake

(Servings: 8, Cooking Time: 40 minutes)

Ingredients:
- 225 g Self Raising
- 150 g Brown Sugar
- 1 Tsp Mixed Spice
- 2 Large Carrots peeled and grated
- 2 Medium Eggs
- 150 ml Olive Oil
- 2 Tbsp Milk
- 50 g Butter
- 1 Small Orange rind and juice
- 235 g Icing Sugar

Directions for Cooking:
1) In blender, blend all wet Ingredients. Add all dry Ingredients: except for carrots and icing sugar and orange. Mix well. Stir in carrots with a spatula.
2) Lightly grease baking pan of air fryer with cooking spray. Pour batter.
3) Cover pan with foil.
4) For 20 minutes, cook on 330ºF. Remove foil and cook for 10 minutes. Let it stand for ten minutes in air fryer.
5) In a small bowl whisk well orange juice, rind, and icing sugar.
6) Once cake has cooled, pour icing on top and spread.
7) Serve and enjoy.

Nutrition Information:
Calories: 529; Carbs: 71.0g; Protein: 5.0g; Fat: 25.0g

Delightful Caramel Cheesecake

(Servings: 8, Cooking Time: 40 minutes)

Ingredients:
- 6 Digestives, crumbled
- 50 g Melted Butter
- 1 Can Dulce de Leche
- 500 g Soft Cheese
- 250 g Caster Sugar
- 4 Large Eggs
- 1 Tbsp Vanilla Essence
- 1 Tbsp Melted Chocolate

Directions for Cooking:
1) Lightly grease baking pan of air fryer with cooking spray. Mix and press crumbled digestives and melted butter on pan bottom. Spread dulce de leche.
2) In bowl, beat well soft cheese and sugar until fluffy. Stir in vanilla and egg. Pour over dulce de leche.
3) Cover pan with foil. For 15 minutes, cook on 390ºF.
4) Cook for 10 minutes at 330ºF. And then 15 minutes at 300ºF.
5) Let it cool completely in air fryer. Refrigerate for at least 4 hours before slicing.
6) Serve and enjoy.

Nutrition Information:
Calories: 463; Carbs: 44.1g; Protein: 17.9g; Fat: 23.8g

Tangy Orange-Choco cake

(Servings: 8, Cooking Time: 35 minutes)

Ingredients:
- 100 g Self Raising Flour
- 110 g Caster Sugar
- 50 g Butter
- 20 g Cocoa Powder
- 1 Tsp Cocoa Nibs
- 1 Large Orange juice and rind
- 1 Tbsp Honey
- 1 Tsp Vanilla Essence
- 2 Medium Eggs
- 50 ml Whole Milk

Frosting Ingredients:
- 50 g Butter
- 100 g Icing Sugar
- 50 ml Orange Juice

Directions for Cooking:

1) In blender, blend all wet Ingredients. Add dry ingredients and blend until smooth.
2) Lightly grease baking pan of air fryer with cooking spray. Pour in batter. Cover pan with foil.
3) For 20 minutes, cook on 330°F. Remove foil and cook for another 10 minutes. Let it stand in air fryer for 5 minutes more.
4) Meanwhile, mix well all frosting ingredients in a bowl. Once cake has cooled, spread on top of cake.
5) Serve and enjoy.

Nutrition Information:
Calories: 284; Carbs: 41.0g; Protein: 3.0g; Fat: 12.0g

Amazing with Every Bite Fried Bananas

(Servings: 4, Cooking Time: 12 minutes)

Ingredients:
- 4 Ripe Bananas, peeled and sliced in half crosswise and then in half lengthwise
- 2 tablespoons All Purpose Flour (Maida)
- 2 tablespoons Rice flour
- 2 tablespoons Corn flour
- 2 tablespoons Desiccated Coconut Powder
- 1 pinch Salt
- 1/2 teaspoon Baking powder

Directions for Cooking:

1) Make the batter by mixing coconut, salt, baking powder, corn flour, rice flour, and Maida in a bowl. Add bananas and cover well in mixture.
2) Lightly grease air fryer basket with cooking spray. Add bananas.
3) For 12 minutes, cook on 390°F. Halfway through cooking time, shake basket.
4) Serve and enjoy.

Nutrition Information:
Calories: 192; Carbs: 32.0g; Protein: 2.1g; Fat: 6.2g

Blackberry-Goodness Cobbler

(Servings: 5, Cooking Time: 20 minutes)

Ingredients:
- 1/4 cup white sugar
- 1 tablespoon cornstarch
- 3 cups fresh blackberries
- 2 tablespoons melted butter
- 1-1/4 cups all-purpose flour
- 3/4 cup white sugar
- 1-1/2 teaspoons baking powder
- 1/2 teaspoon salt
- 1 cup milk
- 1-1/2 teaspoons vanilla extract
- 2 tablespoons melted butter

Directions for Cooking:
1) Lightly grease baking pan of air fryer with cooking spray. Add blackberries and drizzle with 2 tbsps. melted butter.
2) In a small bowl, whisk cornstarch and 1/4 cup sugar. Sprinkle over blackberries and toss well to coat.
3) In another bowl, whisk well salt, baking powder, and ¾ cup sugar. Stir in 2 tbsps. melted butter, vanilla, and milk. Mix well and pour over berries.
4) For 20 minutes, cook on 390°F or until tops are lightly browned.
5) Serve and enjoy.

Nutrition Information:
Calories: 429; Carbs: 76.4g; Protein: 6.1g; Fat: 10.9g

Appetizing Apple Pound Cake

(Servings: 6, Cooking Time: 60 minutes)

Ingredients:
- 1 cup white sugar
- 3/4 cup vegetable oil
- 1 teaspoon vanilla extract
- 1-1/2 eggs
- 1-1/2 cups all-purpose flour
- 1/2 teaspoon baking soda
- 1/4 teaspoon ground cinnamon
- 1/2 teaspoon salt
- 1 medium Granny Smith apples - peeled, cored and chopped
- 2/3 cup and 1 tablespoon chopped walnuts

Directions for Cooking:
1) In blender, blend all Ingredients: except for apples and walnuts. Blend thoroughly. Fold in apples and walnuts.
2) Lightly grease baking pan of air fryer with cooking spray. Pour batter.
3) Cover pan with foil.
4) For 30 minutes, cook on preheated 330°F air fryer.
5) Remove foil and cook for another 20 minutes.
6) Let it stand for 10 minutes.
7) Serve and enjoy.

Nutrition Information:
Calories: 696; Carbs: 71.1g; Protein: 6.5g; Fat: 42.8g

Sugared Doughs with Choco Dip

(Servings: 10, Cooking Time: 24 minutes)

Ingredients:
- 1-pound bread dough, defrosted
- ½ cup butter, melted
- ¾ to 1 cup sugar
- 1 cup heavy cream
- 12 ounces good quality semi-sweet chocolate chips
- 2 tablespoons Amaretto liqueur (or almond extract)

Directions for Cooking:
1) Roll the dough into two 15-inch logs. Cut each log into 20 slices. Cut each slice in half and twist the dough halves together 3 to 4 times. Place the twisted dough on a cookie sheet, brush with melted butter and sprinkle sugar over the dough twists.
2) Lightly grease air fryer basket with cooking spray. Add dough twists in a single layer. Cook in batches for 8 minutes at 390°F. Halfway through cooking time, shake basket and brush with butter. Once done cooking dip in a bowl of sugar.
3) Meanwhile make the dip by heating cream in microwave. Stir in chocolate and heat again until melted and thoroughly combined. Stir in amaretto. And set aside for dipping.
4) Serve and enjoy.

Nutrition Information:
Calories: 469; Carbs: 51.1g; Protein: 5.7g; Fat: 26.8g

Appealingly Coconut-y Cake

(Servings: 8, Cooking Time: 40 minutes)

Ingredients:
- 1 cup gluten-free flour
- 3/4 cup white sugar
- 1/2 cup flaked coconut
- 1/4 cup chopped walnuts
- 1-1/2 teaspoons baking powder
- 1/2 teaspoon baking soda
- 1/2 teaspoon xanthan gum
- 1/2 teaspoon salt
- 1/2 cup coconut milk
- 1/2 cup vegetable oil
- 2 eggs
- 1/2 teaspoon vanilla extract

Directions for Cooking:
1) In blender blend all wet Ingredients. Add dry Ingredients: and blend thoroughly.
2) Lightly grease baking pan of air fryer with cooking spray.
3) Pour in batter. Cover pan with foil.
4) For 30 minutes, cook on 330°F.
5) Let it rest for 10 minutes
6) Serve and enjoy.

Nutrition Information:
Calories: 359; Carbs: 35.2g; Protein: 4.3g; Fat: 22.3g

Cranberry Bread Pudding

(Servings: 4, Cooking Time: 45 minutes)

Ingredients:
- 1-1/2 cups milk
- 3/4 cup heavy whipping cream
- 1/4 cup and 2 tablespoons white sugar
- 2-1/2 eggs
- 3/4 teaspoon lemon zest
- 3/4 teaspoon kosher salt
- 1/8 teaspoon ground cinnamon
- 3/8 vanilla bean, split and seeds scraped away
- 3/4 French baguettes, cut into 2-inch slices
- 1/4 cup golden raisins
- 1/2 cup cranberries1 teaspoon butter

Directions for Cooking:
1) Lightly grease baking pan of air fryer with cooking spray. Spread baguette slices, cranberries, and raisins.
2) In blender, blend well vanilla bean, cinnamon, salt, lemon zest, eggs, sugar, and cream. Pour over baguette slices. Let it soak for an hour.
3) Cover pan with foil.
4) For 35 minutes, cook on 330°F.
5) Let it rest for 10 minutes.
6) Serve and enjoy.

Nutrition Information:
Calories: 581; Carbs: 76.1g; Protein: 15.8g; Fat: 23.7g

Luscious Strawberry Cobbler

(Servings: 4, Cooking Time: 25 minutes)

Ingredients:
- 1/4 cup white sugar
- 1-1/2 teaspoons cornstarch
- 1/2 cup water
- 1-1/2 cups strawberries, hulled
- 1 tablespoon butter, diced
- 1/2 cup all-purpose flour
- 1-1/2 teaspoons white sugar
- 3/4 teaspoon baking powder
- 1/4 teaspoon salt
- 1 tablespoon and 2 teaspoons butter
- 1/4 cup heavy whipping cream

Directions for Cooking:
1) Lightly grease baking pan of air fryer with cooking spray. Add water, cornstarch, and sugar. Cook for 10 minutes 390°F or until hot and thick. Add strawberries and mix well. Dot tops with 1 tbsp butter.
2) In a bowl, mix well salt, baking powder, sugar, and flour. Cut in 1 tbsp and 2 tsp butter. Mix in cream. Spoon on top of berries.
3) Cook for 15 minutes at 390°F, until tops are lightly browned.
4) Serve and enjoy.

Nutrition Information:
Calories: 255; Carbs: 32.0g; Protein: 2.4g; Fat: 13.0g

Air Fryed Churros with Choco Dip

(Servings: 12, Cooking Time: 30 minutes)

Ingredients:
- 1/2 cup water
- 1/4 teaspoon kosher salt
- 1/4 cup , plus 2 Tbsp. unsalted butter, divided
- 1/2 cup (about 2 1/8 oz.) all-purpose flour
- 2 large eggs
- 1/3 cup granulated sugar
- 2 teaspoons ground cinnamon
- 4 ounces bittersweet baking chocolate, finely chopped
- 3 tablespoons heavy cream
- 2 tablespoons vanilla kefir

Directions for Cooking:
1) In small saucepan, bring to a boil ¼ cup butter, salt, and water. Stir in flour and lower fire to a simmer. Cook until smooth and thickened and pulls away from side of pan.
2) Transfer dough to a bowl and stir constantly until cooled.
3) Stir in eggs one at a time.
4) Transfer to a pastry bag with a star tip. Chill for half an hour.
5) Lightly grease baking pan of air fryer with cooking spray. Pipe dough on bottom of pan in 3-inch lengths.
6) For 10 minutes, cook on 390°F. Halfway through cooking time, shake. Cook in batches
7) In a small bowl mix cinnamon and sugar. In another bowl, place melted butter.
8) Brush cooked churros with melted butter and then roll in sugar mixture.
9) In microwave safe bowl, melt cream and chocolate. Mix well and stir in vanilla.
10) Serve and enjoy with dip on the side.

Nutrition Information:
Calories: 159; Carbs: 12.0g; Protein: 3.0g; Fat: 11.0g

Out-of-this-World PB&J Doughnuts

(Servings: 6, Cooking Time: 30 minutes)

Ingredients:
- 1 1/4 Cups all-purpose flour
- 1/3 Cup sugar
- 1/2 Teaspoon baking powder
- 1/2 Teaspoon baking soda
- 3/4 Teaspoon salt
- 1 Egg
- 1/2 Cup buttermilk
- 1 Teaspoon vanilla
- 2 Tablespoons unsalted butter, melted and cooled
- 1 Tablespoon melted butter for brushing the tops

Filling Ingredient:
- 1/2 Cup Blueberry or strawberry jelly (not preserves)

Glaze Ingredients:
- 1/2 Cup powdered sugar
- 2 Tablespoons milk
- 2 Tablespoons peanut butter
- Pinch of sea salt

Directions for Cooking:
1) In mixing bowl, whisk well all wet Ingredients. Mix in dry Ingredients: and beat until thoroughly combined.

Roll dough to ¾-inch thickness. Cut into 3.5-inch rounds.
2) Lightly grease baking pan of air fryer with cooking spray. Add doughnuts in single layer. Cook in batches at for 10 minutes at 330°F.
3) Meanwhile, make the glaze by mixing all Ingredients: in a bowl.
4) Fill each doughnut with filling and spread glaze on top.
5) Serve and enjoy.

Nutrition Information:
Calories: 243; Carbs: 37.6g; Protein: 5.7g; Fat: 7.7g

Enchanting Coffee-Apple Cake
(Servings: 6, Cooking Time: 40 minutes)

Ingredients:
- 2 tablespoons butter, softened
- 1/4 cup and 2 tablespoons brown sugar
- 1/2 large egg
- 2 tablespoons sour cream
- 2 tablespoons vanilla yogurt
- 1/2 teaspoon vanilla extract
- 1/2 cup all-purpose flour
- 1/4 teaspoon ground cinnamon
- 1/4 teaspoon baking soda
- 1/8 teaspoon salt
- 1 cup diced Granny Smith apple

Topping Ingredients:
- 2 tablespoons brown sugar
- 2 tablespoons all-purpose flour
- 1 tablespoon butter
- 1/4 teaspoon ground cinnamon

Directions for Cooking:
1) In blender, puree all wet Ingredients. Add dry Ingredients: except for apples and blend until smooth. Stir in apples.
2) Lightly grease baking pan of air fryer with cooking spray. Pour batter into pan.
3) In a small bowl mix well, all topping Ingredients: and spread on top of cake batter.
4) Cover pan with foil.
5) For 20 minutes, cook on 330°F.
6) Remove foil and cook for 10 minutes. Let it stand in air fryer for another 10 minutes.
7) Serve and enjoy.

Nutrition Information:
Calories: 279; Carbs: 41.4g; Protein: 3.6g; Fat: 11.0g

Pumpkin Pie in Air Fryer

(Servings: 8, Cooking Time: 35 minutes)

Ingredients:
- 1 (15 ounce) can pumpkin puree
- 3 egg yolks
- 1 large egg
- 1 (14 ounce) can sweetened condensed milk
- 1 teaspoon ground cinnamon
- 1/2 teaspoon ground ginger
- 1/2 teaspoon fine salt
- 1/4 teaspoon freshly grated nutmeg
- 1/8 teaspoon Chinese 5-spice powder
- 1 9-inch unbaked pie crust

Directions for Cooking:
1) Lightly grease baking pan of air fryer with cooking spray. Press pie crust on bottom of pan, stretching all the way up to the sides of the pan. Pierce all over with fork.
2) In blender, blend well egg, egg yolks, and pumpkin puree. Add Chinese 5-spice powder, nutmeg, salt, ginger, cinnamon, and condensed milk. Pour on top of pie crust.
3) Cover pan with foil.
4) For 15 minutes, cook on preheated 390°F air fryer.
5) Remove foil and continue cooking for 20 minutes at 330°F until middle is set.
6) Allow to cool in air fryer completely.
7) Serve and enjoy.

Nutrition Information:
Calories: 326; Carbs: 41.9g; Protein: 7.6g; Fat: 14.2g

Easy 'n Delicious Brownies

(Servings: 8, Cooking Time: 20 minutes)

Ingredients:
- 1/4 cup butter
- 1/2 cup white sugar
- 1 egg
- 1/2 teaspoon vanilla extract
- 2 tablespoons and 2 teaspoons unsweetened cocoa powder
- 1/4 cup all-purpose flour
- 1/8 teaspoon salt
- 1/8 teaspoon baking powder

Frosting Ingredients:
- 1 tablespoon and 1-1/2 teaspoons butter, softened
- 1 tablespoon and 1-1/2 teaspoons unsweetened cocoa powder
- 1-1/2 teaspoons honey
- 1/2 teaspoon vanilla extract
- 1/2 cup confectioners' sugar

Directions for Cooking:
1) Lightly grease baking pan of air fryer with cooking spray. Melt ¼ cup butter for 3 minutes. Stir in vanilla, eggs, and sugar. Mix well.
2) Stir in baking powder, salt, flour, and cocoa mix well. Evenly spread.
3) For 20 minutes, cook on 300°F.
4) In a small bowl, make the frosting by mixing well all Ingredients. Frost brownies while still warm.
5) Serve and enjoy.

Nutrition Information:
Calories: 191; Carbs: 25.7g; Protein: 1.8g; Fat: 9.0g

Skewer Recipes

Chicken and Pineapple BBQ

(Servings: 5, Cooking Time: 20 minutes)

Ingredients:
- 1/2 cup pineapple juice
- 1/4 cup packed brown sugar
- 3 tablespoons light soy sauce
- 1-pound chicken breast tenderloins or strips

Directions for Cooking:
1) In a small saucepan bring to a boil pineapple juice, brown sugar, and soy sauce. Transfer to a large bowl. Stir in chicken and pineapple. Let it marinate in the fridge for an hour.
2) Thread pineapple and chicken in skewers. Place on skewer rack.
3) For 10 minutes, cook on 360°F. Halfway through cooking time, turnover chicken and baste with marinade.
4) Serve and enjoy.

Nutrition Information:
Calories: 157; Carbs: 14.7g; Protein: 19.4g; Fat: 2.2g

Sweetly Honeyed Chicken Kebabs

(Servings: 8, Cooking Time: 36 minutes)

Ingredients:
- 2 tablespoons vegetable oil
- 2 tablespoons and 2 teaspoons honey
- 2 tablespoons and 2 teaspoons soy sauce
- 1/8 teaspoon ground black pepper
- 4 skinless, boneless chicken breast halves cut into 1-inch cubes
- 1 clove garlic
- 2-1/2 small onions, cut into 2-inch pieces
- 1 red bell peppers, cut into 2-inch pieces

Directions for Cooking:
1) Whisk well pepper, soy sauce, honey, and oil. Transfer ¼ of the marinade to a small bowl for basting. Add chicken to bowl and toss well to coat. Add pepper, onion, and garlic. Toss well to mix. Let it marinate for 2 hours.
2) Thread vegetables and chicken into skewers and place on sewer rack in air fryer.
3) For 12 minutes, cook on 360°F. Halfway through cooking time, baste with marinade sauce and turnover skewers.
4) Serve and enjoy.

Nutrition Information:
Calories: 179; Carbs: 12.4g; Protein: 17.4g; Fat: 6.6g

Skewered Beef Asian Way

(Servings: 3, Cooking Time: 5 minutes)

Ingredients:
- 1 tablespoon and 1-1/2 teaspoons hoisin sauce
- 1 tablespoon and 1-1/2 teaspoons sherry
- 2 tablespoons soy sauce
- 1/2 teaspoon barbeque sauce
- 1 green onions, chopped
- 1 clove garlic, minced
- 1-1/2 teaspoons minced fresh ginger root
- 3/4-pound flank steak, thinly sliced

Directions for Cooking:

1) In a resealable bag, mix well ginger, garlic, green onions, barbecue sauce, soy sauce, sherry, and hoisin. Add steak and mix well. Remove excess air, seal, and marinate for at least 2 hours.
2) Thread steak into skewers and discard marinade.
3) For 5 minutes, cook on preheated 390°F air fryer.
4) Serve and enjoy.

Nutrition Information:
Calories: 130; Carbs: 6.7g; Protein: 14.7g; Fat: 4.9g

Teriyaki 'n Hawaiian Chicken

(Servings: 4, Cooking Time: 23 minutes)

Ingredients:
- 2 boneless skinless chicken breasts, cut into 1-inch cubes
- ½ cup brown sugar
- ½ cup soy sauce
- ¼ cup pineapple juice
- 2 garlic cloves, minced
- ¼ teaspoon pepper
- ½ teaspoon salt
- 1 Tablespoon cornstarch
- 1 Tablespoon water
- 1 red bell pepper, cut into 1-inch cubes
- 1 yellow red bell pepper, cut into 1-inch cubes
- 1 green bell pepper, cut into 1-inch cubes
- 1 red onion, cut into 1-inch cubes
- 2 cups fresh pineapple cut into 1-inch cubes
- green onions, for garnish

Directions for Cooking:

1) In a saucepan, bring to a boil salt, pepper, garlic, pineapple juice, soy sauce, and brown sugar. In a small bowl whisk well, cornstarch and water. Slowly stir in to mixture in pan while whisking constantly. Simmer until thickened, around 3 minutes. Save ¼ cup of the sauce for basting and set aside.
2) In shallow dish, mix well chicken and remaining thickened sauce. Toss well to coat. Marinate in the ref for a half hour.
3) Thread bell pepper, onion, pineapple, and chicken pieces in skewers. Place on skewer rack in air fryer.
4) For 10 minutes, cook on 360°F. Halfway through cooking time, turnover skewers and baste with sauce. If needed, cook in batches.
5) Serve and enjoy with a sprinkle of green onions.

Nutrition Information:
Calories: 391; Carbs: 58.7g; Protein: 31.2g; Fat: 3.4g

Chicken Kebabs Greek Way

(Servings: 4, Cooking Time: 24 minutes)

Ingredients:
- 1 (8 ounce) container fat-free plain yogurt
- 1/3 cup crumbled feta cheese with basil and sun-dried tomatoes
- 1/2 teaspoon lemon zest
- 2 tablespoons fresh lemon juice
- 2 teaspoons dried oregano
- 1/2 teaspoon salt
- 1/4 teaspoon ground black pepper
- 1/4 teaspoon crushed dried rosemary
- 1-pound skinless, boneless chicken breast halves - cut into 1-inch pieces
- 1 large red onion, cut into wedges
- 1 large green bell pepper, cut into 1 1/2-inch pieces

Directions for Cooking:
1) In a shallow dish, mix well rosemary, pepper, salt, oregano, lemon juice, lemon zest, feta cheese, and yogurt. Add chicken and toss well to coat. Marinate in the ref for 3 hours.
2) Thread bell pepper, onion, and chicken pieces in skewers. Place on skewer rack.
3) For 12 minutes, cook on 360°F. Halfway through cooking time, turnover skewers. If needed, cook in batches.
4) Serve and enjoy.

Nutrition Information:
Calories: 242; Carbs: 12.3g; Protein: 31.0g; Fat: 7.5g

Skewered Oriental Teriyaki Beef

(Servings: 6, Cooking Time: 12 minutes)

Ingredients:
- 1/4 cup and 2 tablespoons light brown sugar
- 1/4 cup soy sauce
- 2 tablespoons pineapple juice (optional)
- 2 tablespoons water
- 1 tablespoon vegetable oil
- 3/4 large garlic cloves, chopped
- 1-pound boneless round steak, cut into 1/4-inch slices

Directions for Cooking:

1) In a resealable bag, mix all Ingredients: thoroughly except for beef. Then add beef, remove excess air, and seal. Place in ref and marinate for at least a day.
2) Thread beef into skewers and place on skewer rack in air fryer. If needed, cook in batches.
3) For 6 minutes, cook on 390°F.
4) Serve and enjoy.

Nutrition Information:
Calories: 191; Carbs: 15.2g; Protein: 15.9g; Fat: 7.4g

Grilled Beef with Ginger-Hoisin

(Servings: 5, Cooking Time: 16 minutes)

Ingredients:
- 1-pound flank steak, sliced at an angle 1" x ¼" thick
- 1/4 cup hoisin sauce
- 1 tablespoon lime juice
- 1-1/2 teaspoons honey
- 1/2 clove garlic, minced
- 1/2 teaspoon kosher salt
- 1/2 teaspoon peeled and grated fresh ginger root
- 1/2 teaspoon sesame oil (optional)
- 1/2 teaspoon chile-garlic sauce (such as Sriracha®)
- 1/4 teaspoon crushed red pepper flakes
- 1/8 teaspoon ground black pepper
- 1-1/2 teaspoons toasted sesame seeds
- 1 chopped green onions

Directions for Cooking:
1) In a shallow dish, mix well pepper, red pepper flakes, chile-garlic sauce, sesame oil, ginger, salt, honey, lime juice, and hoisin sauce. Add steak and toss well to coat. Marinate in the ref for 3 hours.
2) Thread steak in skewers. Place on skewer rack in air fryer.
3) For 8 minutes, cook on 360°F. If needed, cook in batches.
4) Serve and enjoy with a drizzle of green onions and sesame seeds.

Nutrition Information:
Calories: 123; Carbs: 8.3g; Protein: 11.7g; Fat: 4.7g

Spiced Lime 'n Coconut Shrimp Skewer

(Servings: 6, Cooking Time: 12 minutes)

Ingredients:
- 2 jalapeno peppers, seeded
- 1 lime, zested and juiced
- 2 garlic cloves
- 1/3 cup chopped fresh cilantro
- 1/3 cup shredded coconut
- 1/4 cup olive oil
- 1/4 cup soy sauce
- 1-pound uncooked medium shrimp, peeled and deveined

Directions for Cooking:
1) In food processor, process until smooth the soy sauce, olive oil, coconut oil, cilantro, garlic, lime juice, lime zest, and jalapeno.
2) In a shallow dish, mix well shrimp and processed marinade. Toss well to coat and marinate in the ref for 3 hours.
3) Thread shrimps in skewers. Place on skewer rack in air fryer.
4) For 6 minutes, cook on 360°F. If needed, cook in batches.
5) Serve and enjoy.

Nutrition Information:
Calories: 172; Carbs: 4.8g; Protein: 13.4g; Fat: 10.9g

Tangy Grilled Fig-Prosciutto

(Servings: 2, Cooking Time: 8 minutes)

Ingredients:
- 2 whole figs, sliced in quarters
- 8 prosciutto slices
- Pepper and salt to taste

Directions for Cooking:
1) Wrap a prosciutto slice around one slice of fid and then thread into skewer. Repeat process for remaining Ingredients. Place on skewer rack in air fryer.
2) For 8 minutes, cook on 390°F. Halfway through cooking time, turnover skewers.
3) Serve and enjoy.

Nutrition Information:
Calories: 277; Carbs: 10.7g; Protein: 36.0g; Fat: 10.0g

Veggie Souvlaki on Air Fryer Grill

(Servings: 2, Cooking Time: 20 minutes)

Ingredients:
- 3 garlic cloves
- 1 tablespoon coriander seeds
- 1 tablespoon olive oil
- 1 teaspoon cumin
- 1 teaspoon paprika
- 1 teaspoon salt
- 1 zucchini, sliced into 1-inch thick circles
- 1 Chinese eggplant, sliced into 1-inch thick circles
- 1 medium bell pepper, cut into chunks

Directions for Cooking:
1) In a food processor, process garlic, coriander, olive oil, cumin, paprika, and salt until creamy.
2) Thread bell pepper, eggplant, and zucchini in skewers. Brush with garlic creamy paste. Place on skewer rack in air fryer.
3) For 10 minutes, cook on 360°F. Halfway through cooking time, turnover skewers. If needed, cook in batches.
4) Serve and enjoy.

Nutrition Information:
Calories: 181; Carbs: 22.4g; Protein: 4.2g; Fat: 8.2g

Swordfish with Sage on the Grill

(Servings: 2, Cooking Time: 16 minutes)

Ingredients:
- 1/2-pound swordfish, sliced into 2-inch chunks
- 1 tbsp lemon juice
- 1 tsp parsley
- salt and pepper to taste.
- 1 zucchini, peeled and then thinly sliced in lengths

- 2 tbsp olive oil
- ½ lemon, sliced thinly in rounds
- 6-8 sage leaves

Directions for Cooking:
1) In a shallow dish, mix well lemon juice, parsley, and sliced swordfish. Toss well to coat and generously season with pepper and salt. Marinate for at least 10 minutes.
2) Place one length of zucchini on a flat surface. Add one piece of fish and sage leaf. Roll zucchini and then thread into a skewer. Repeat process to remaining Ingredients.
3) Brush with oil and place on skewer rack in air fryer.
4) For 8 minutes, cook on 390°F. If needed, cook in batches.
5) Serve and enjoy with lemon slices.

Nutrition Information:
Calories: 297; Carbs: 3.7g; Protein: 22.8g; Fat: 21.2g

Scallops and Bacon Grill

(Servings: 2, Cooking Time: 12 minutes)

Ingredients:
- 6 large scallops
- 6 bacon strips
- 1 teaspoon smoked paprika

Directions for Cooking:
1) Wrap one bacon around one scallop and thread in a skewer ensuring that it will not unravel. Repeat until all Ingredients: are used.
2) Season with paprika.
3) Place on skewer rack in air fryer.
4) For 12 minutes, cook on 390°F. Halfway through cooking time, turnover skewers.
5) Serve and enjoy.

Nutrition Information:
Calories: 72; Carbs: 2.4g; Protein: 1.9g; Fat: 6.0g

Grilled Chipotle Shrimp

(Servings: 2, Cooking Time: 24 minutes)

Ingredients:
- 1/4 cup barbecue sauce
- juice of 1/2 orange
- 3 tablespoons minced chipotles in adobo sauce
- salt
- ½-pound large shrimps

Directions for Cooking:
1) In a small shallow dish, mix well all Ingredients: except for shrimp. Save ¼ of the mixture for basting.
2) Add shrimp in dish and toss well to coat. Marinate for at least 10 minutes.
3) Thread shrimps in skewers. Place on skewer rack in air fryer.
4) For 12 minutes, cook on 360°F. Halfway through cooking time, turnover skewers and baste with sauce. If needed, cook in batches.
5) Serve and enjoy.

Nutrition Information:
Calories: 179; Carbs: 24.6g; Protein: 16.6g; Fat: 1.5g

Grilled Chicken Shish Tanoak

(Servings: 3, Cooking Time: 20 minutes)

Ingredients:
- 2 tablespoons lemon juice
- 2 tablespoons vegetable oil
- 1/3 cup plain yogurt
- 2 cloves garlic, minced
- 1 teaspoon tomato paste
- 3/4 teaspoon salt
- 1/2 teaspoon dried oregano
- 1/8 teaspoon ground black pepper
- 1/8 teaspoon ground allspice
- 1/8 teaspoon ground cinnamon
- 1/8 teaspoon ground cardamom
- 1-pound skinless, boneless chicken breast halves cut into 2-inch pieces
- 1 onion, cut into large chunks
- 1 small green bell pepper, cut into large chunks
- 1/2 cup chopped fresh flat-leaf parsley

Directions for Cooking:
1) In a resealable plastic bag, mix cardamom, cinnamon, allspice, pepper, oregano, salt, tomato paste, garlic, yogurt, vegetable oil, and lemon juice. Add chicken, remove excess air, seal, and marinate in the ref for at least 4 hours.
2) Thread chicken into skewers, place on skewer rack and cook in batches.
3) For 10 minutes, cook on 360°F. Halfway through cooking time, turnover skewers.
4) Serve and enjoy with a sprinkle of parsley.

Nutrition Information:
Calories: 297; Carbs: 9.8g; Protein: 34.3g; Fat: 13.4g

Beef Eastern Shish Kebabs

(Servings: 4, Cooking Time: 20 minutes)

Ingredients:
- 1/3 cup vegetable oil
- 1/2 cup soy sauce
- 1/4 cup lemon juice
- 1 tablespoon prepared mustard
- 1 tablespoon Worcestershire sauce
- 1 clove garlic, minced
- 1 teaspoon coarsely cracked black pepper
- 1 1/2 teaspoons salt
- 1 1/2 pounds lean beef, cut into 1-inch cubes
- 16 mushroom caps
- 2 green bell peppers, cut into chunks
- 1 red bell pepper, cut into chunks
- 1 large onion, cut into large squares

Directions for Cooking:
1) In a resealable bag, mix well salt, pepper, garlic, Worcestershire, mustard, lemon juice, soy sauce, and oil. Add beef and toss well to coat. Remove excess air and seal. Marinate for 8 hours. Add mushroom and marinate for an additional 8 hours.
2) Thread mushrooms, bell peppers, onion, and meat in skewers.
3) Pour marinade in saucepan and thicken for 10 minutes and transfer to a bowl for basting.
4) Place skewers on skewer rack in air fryer. If needed, cook in batches.

5) For 10 minutes, cook on 390°F. Halfway through cooking time, baste and turnover skewers.
6) Serve and enjoy.

Nutrition Information:
Calories: 426; Carbs: 15.8g; Protein: 26.2g; Fat: 28.6g

Dill-Rubbed Grilled Salmon

(Servings: 2, Cooking Time: 12 minutes)

Ingredients:
- 1-lb salmon filet, cut into 2-inch rectangles
- 3 tablespoons hoisin sauce
- 1 tablespoon soy sauce
- 1 tablespoon rice wine
- 1 tablespoon honey
- 1 tablespoon olive oil

Directions for Cooking:
1) In a shallow dish, mix well all Ingredients. Marinate in the ref for 3 hours.
2) Thread salmon pieces in skewers and reserve marinade for basting. Place on skewer rack in air fryer.
3) For 12 minutes, cook on 360°F. Halfway through cooking time, turnover skewers and baste with marinade. If needed, cook in batches.
4) Serve and enjoy.

Nutrition Information:
Calories: 971; Carbs: 23.0g; Protein: 139.4g; Fat: 35.7g

Turkey Meatballs in Skewer

(Servings: 4, Cooking Time: 25 minutes)

Ingredients:
- 1/3 cup cranberry sauce
- 1 1/2 tablespoons barbecue sauce
- 1 ½ tablespoons water
- 2 teaspoons cider vinegar
- 1 tsp salt and more to taste
- 1-pound ground turkey
- 1/4-pound ground bacon

Directions for Cooking:
1) In a bowl, mix well with hands the turkey, ground bacon and a tsp of salt. Evenly form into 16 equal sized balls.
2) In a small saucepan boil cranberry sauce, barbecue sauce, water, cider vinegar, and a dash or two of salt. Mix well and simmer for 3 minutes.
3) Thread meatballs in skewers and baste with cranberry sauce. Place on skewer rack in air fryer.
4) For 15 minutes, cook on 360°F. Every after 5 minutes of cooking time, turnover skewers and baste with sauce. If needed, cook in batches.
5) Serve and enjoy.

Nutrition Information:
Calories: 217; Carbs: 11.5g; Protein: 28.0g; Fat: 10.9g

Grilled Curried Chicken

(Servings: 3, Cooking Time: 12 minutes)

Ingredients:
- 2/3 cup coconut milk
- 3 tablespoons peanut butter
- 1 tablespoon Thai curry paste
- 1 tablespoon lime juice
- 1 teaspoon salt
- ½-lb boneless and skinless chicken thigh meat, cut into 2-inch chunks
- 1 medium bell pepper, seeded and cut into chunks

Directions for Cooking:
1) In a shallow dish, mix well all Ingredients: except for chicken and bell pepper. Transfer half of the sauce in a small bowl for basting.
2) Add chicken to dish and toss well to coat. Marinate in the ref for 3 hours.
3) Thread bell pepper and chicken pieces in skewers. Place on skewer rack in air fryer.
4) For 12 minutes, cook on 360°F. Halfway through cooking time, turnover skewers and baste with sauce. If needed, cook in batches.
5) Serve and enjoy.

Nutrition Information:
Calories: 282; Carbs: 10.0g; Protein: 20.0g; Fat: 18.0g

Cajun Pork on the Grill

(Servings: 3, Cooking Time: 12 minutes)

Ingredients:
- 1-lb pork loin, sliced into 1-inch cubes
- 3 tablespoons brown sugar
- 2 tablespoons Cajun seasoning
- 1/4 cup cider vinegar
- ¼ cup brown sugar

Directions for Cooking:
1) In a shallow dish, mix well pork loin, 3 tablespoons brown sugar, and Cajun seasoning. Toss well to coat. Marinate in the ref for 3 hours.
2) In a medium bowl mix well, brown sugar and vinegar for basting.
3) Thread pork pieces in skewers. Baste with sauce and place on skewer rack in air fryer.
4) For 12 minutes, cook on 360°F. Halfway through cooking time, turnover skewers and baste with sauce. If needed, cook in batches.
5) Serve and enjoy.

Nutrition Information:
Calories: 428; Carbs: 30.3g; Protein: 39.0g; Fat: 16.7g

Peppered & Carbonated Sirloin Kebabs

(Servings: 4, Cooking Time: 20 minutes)

Ingredients:
- 2 tablespoons soy sauce
- 1 1/2 tablespoons light brown sugar
- 1 1/2 tablespoon distilled white vinegar
- 1/4 teaspoon garlic powder
- 1/4 teaspoon seasoned salt
- 1/4 teaspoon garlic pepper seasoning
- 1/4 cup lemon-lime flavored carbonated beverage
- 1-pound beef sirloin steak, cut into 1 1/2-inch cubes
- 1 green bell peppers, cut into 2-inch pieces
- 1/4-pound fresh mushrooms, stems removed
- 1 cup cherry tomatoes
- 1/2 fresh pineapple - peeled, cored and cubed

Directions for Cooking:

1) Whisk well carbonated beverage, garlic pepper seasoning, seasoned salt, garlic powder, white vinegar, light brown sugar, and soy sauce. Transfer ¼ cup to a bowl for basting. Place remaining sauce in a Ziploc bag.
2) Add steak in bag and marinate for at least overnight. Ensuring to turnover at least twice.
3) Thread pineapple, tomatoes, mushrooms, green peppers, and steak in skewers. Place on skewer rack on air fryer. Cook in batches. Baste with reserved sauce.
4) For 10 minutes, cook on 360°F. Halfway through cooking time, baste and turnover skewers.
5) Serve and enjoy.

Nutrition Information:
Calories: 330; Carbs: 19.2g; Protein: 24.0g; Fat: 17.4g

Grilled Jerk Chicken

(Servings: 2, Cooking Time: 30 minutes)

Ingredients:
- 2 whole chicken thighs
- ¼ cup pineapple chunks
- 4 tablespoons jerk seasoning
- 1 tablespoon vegetable oil
- 3 teaspoons lime juice

Directions for Cooking:
1) In a shallow dish, mix well all Ingredients. Marinate in the ref for 3 hours.
2) Thread chicken pieces and pineapples in skewers. Place on skewer rack in air fryer.
3) For 30 minutes, cook on 360°F. Halfway through cooking time, turnover skewers.
4) Serve and enjoy.

Nutrition Information:
Calories: 579; Carbs: 36.3g; Protein: 25.7g; Fat: 36.7g

Chicken Caesar on the Grill

(Servings: 3, Cooking Time: 24 minutes)

Ingredients:
- 1-pound ground chicken
- 2 tablespoons Caesar dressing and more for drizzling
- 1/2 cup Parmesan
- 1/4 cup breadcrumbs
- 1 teaspoon lemon zest. Form into ovals, skewer and grill.
- 2-4 romaine leaves
- ¼ cup crouton

Directions for Cooking:
1) In a shallow dish, mix well chicken, 2 tablespoons Caesar dressing, parmesan, and breadcrumbs. Mix well with hands. Form into 1-inch oval patties.
2) Thread chicken pieces in skewers. Place on skewer rack in air fryer.
3) For 12 minutes, cook on 360°F. Halfway through cooking time, turnover skewers. If needed, cook in batches.
4) Serve and enjoy on a bed of lettuce and sprinkle with croutons and extra dressing.

Nutrition Information:
Calories: 339; Carbs: 9.5g; Protein: 32.6g; Fat: 18.9g

Rosemary-Rubbed Grilled Lamb

(Servings: 2, Cooking Time: 12 minutes)

Ingredients:
- 1-lb cubed lamb leg
- 1/2 cup olive oil
- juice of 1 lemon
- fresh rosemary
- 3 smashed garlic cloves
- salt and pepper

Directions for Cooking:
1) In a shallow dish, mix well all Ingredients: and marinate for 3 hours.
2) Thread lamb pieces in skewers. Place on skewer rack in air fryer.
3) For 12 minutes, cook on 390°F. Halfway through cooking time, turnover skewers. If needed, cook in batches.
4) Serve and enjoy.

Nutrition Information:
Calories: 560; Carbs: 5.4g; Protein: 46.5g; Fat: 39.1g

Thai-Style Grilled Pork

(Servings: 3, Cooking Time: 15 minutes)

Ingredients:
- 1-pound ground pork
- 3 tablespoons chopped mint
- 3 tablespoons cilantro
- 3 tablespoons basil
- 1 minced shallot
- 1 minced hot chile
- 2 tablespoons fish sauce
- 2 tablespoons lime juice

Directions for Cooking:

1) In a shallow dish, mix well all Ingredients: with hands. Form into 1-inch ovals.
2) Thread ovals in skewers. Place on skewer rack in air fryer.
3) For 15 minutes, cook on 360°F. Halfway through cooking time, turnover skewers. If needed, cook in batches.
4) Serve and enjoy.

Nutrition Information:
Calories: 455; Carbs: 2.5g; Protein: 40.2g; Fat: 31.5g

Hungarian Style Grilled Beef

(Servings: 3, Cooking Time: 12 minutes)

Ingredients:
- 1-lb beef tri-tip, sliced to 2-inch cubes
- 1/2 cup olive oil
- 2 smashed garlic cloves
- a pinch of salt
- 1/2 teaspoon paprika
- 2 teaspoons crushed caraway seeds
- 1 medium red onion, sliced into quarters
- 1 medium bell pepper seeded and cut into chunks

Directions for Cooking:

1) In a shallow dish, mix well all Ingredients: except for bell pepper and onion. Toss well to coat. Marinate in the ref for 3 hours.
2) Thread beef, onion, and bell pepper pieces in skewers. Place on skewer rack in air fryer.
3) For 12 minutes, cook on 360°F. Halfway through cooking time, turnover skewers. If needed, cook in batches.
4) Serve and enjoy.

Nutrition Information:
Calories: 530; Carbs: 3.3g; Protein: 33.1g; Fat: 42.7g

Grilled Buccaneer Pork

(Servings: 3, Cooking Time: 15 minutes)

Ingredients:
- 1 cup water
- 3 tablespoons each salt
- 3 tablespoons brown sugar
- 2 teaspoons pickling spices
- 4 garlic cloves
- 1 cup rum
- 1-lb pork tenderloin, sliced into 1-inch cubes
- ½ cup ready-made jerk sauce

Directions for Cooking:
1) In a saucepan, bring to a boil water salt and brown sugar. Stir in garlic and pickling spices and simmer for 3 minutes. Turn off fire and whisk in rum.
2) Transfer sauce to a shallow dish, mix well pork tenderloin and marinate in the ref for 3 hours.
3) Thread pork pieces in skewers. Baste with jerk sauce and place on skewer rack in air fryer.
4) For 12 minutes, cook on 360°F. Halfway through cooking time, turnover skewers and baste with sauce. If needed, cook in batches.
5) Serve and enjoy.

Nutrition Information:
Calories: 295; Carbs: 19.9g; Protein: 41.0g; Fat: 5.7g

Grilled Steak with Scallion Dip

(Servings: 4, Cooking Time: 20 minutes)

Ingredients:
- 1 cup canned unsweetened coconut milk
- 1/4 cup fish sauce
- 2 tablespoons packed light brown sugar
- 1 tablespoon fresh lime juice
- 6 garlic cloves
- 4 red or green Thai chiles, stemmed
- 2 lemongrass stalks, bottom third only, tough outer layers removed
- 1 1 1/2" piece ginger, peeled
- 1-pound tri-tip fat cap left on , cut into 1-inch cubes

Scallion Dip Ingredients:
- 15 scallions, very thinly sliced
- 1/4 cup fish sauce
- 3 tablespoons grapeseed oil
- 2 tablespoons black vinegar
- 2 tablespoons toasted sesame seeds

Basting Sauce Ingredients:
- 1/2 cup canned unsweetened coconut milk
- 3 tablespoons fish sauce
- 1 1/2 tablespoons fresh lime juice
- 2 garlic cloves, crushed

Directions for Cooking:
1) Except for meat, puree all Ingredients: in a blender. Transfer into a bowl and marinate beef at least overnight in the ref.
2) In a medium bowl, mix well all scallion dip Ingredients: and set aside.
3) In a separate bowl mix all basting sauce Ingredients.

4) Thread meat into skewers and place on skewer rack in air fryer. Baste with sauce.
5) Cook for 10 minutes at 390°F or to desired doneness. Halfway through cooking time, baste and turnover skewers.
6) Serve and enjoy with the dip on the side.

Nutrition Information:
Calories: 579; Carbs: 15.3g; Protein: 32.0g; Fat: 43.3g

Baked Recipes

Orange-Caesar Dressed Roughie

(Servings: 2, Cooking Time: 15 minutes)

Ingredients:
- 2 orange roughie fillets (4 ounces each)
- 1/4 cup creamy Caesar salad dressing
- 1/2 cups crushed butter-flavored crackers
- 1/2 cup shredded cheddar cheese

Directions for Cooking:
1) Lightly grease baking pan of air fryer with cooking spray. Add filet on bottom of pan. Drizzle with dressing, sprinkle crumbled crackers.
2) For 10 minutes, cook on 390°F.
3) Sprinkle cheese and let it stand for 5 minutes.
4) Serve and enjoy.

Nutrition Information:
Calories: 341; Carbs: 5.0g; Protein: 32.6g; Fat: 21.1g

Salmon with Crisped Topped Crumbs

(Servings: 2, Cooking Time: 15 minutes)

Ingredients:
- 1-1/2 cups soft bread crumbs
- 2 tablespoons minced fresh parsley
- 1 tablespoon minced fresh thyme or 1 teaspoon dried thyme
- 2 garlic cloves, minced
- 1 teaspoon grated lemon zest
- 1/2 teaspoon salt
- 1/4 teaspoon lemon-pepper seasoning
- 1/4 teaspoon paprika
- 1 tablespoon butter, melted
- 2 salmon fillets (6 ounces each)

Directions for Cooking:
1) In a medium bowl mix well bread crumbs, fresh parsley thyme, garlic, lemon zest, salt, lemon-pepper seasoning, and paprika.
2) Lightly grease baking pan of air fryer with cooking spray. Add salmon filet with skin side down. Evenly sprinkle crumbs on tops of salmon.
3) For 10 minutes, cook on 390°F. Let it rest for 5 minutes.
4) Serve and enjoy.

Nutrition Information:
Calories: 331; Carbs: 9.0g; Protein: 31.0g; Fat: 19.0g

Orange & Tofu Fry

(Servings: 4, Cooking Time: 25 minutes)

Ingredients:
- 1-pound extra-firm tofu drained and pressed (or use super-firm tofu), cut in cubes
- 1 Tablespoon tamari
- 1 Tablespoon cornstarch (or arrowroot powder)

Sauce Ingredients:
- 1 teaspoon orange zest
- 1/3 cup orange juice
- 1/2 cup water
- 2 teaspoons cornstarch (or arrowroot powder)
- 1/4 teaspoon crushed red pepper flakes
- 1 teaspoon fresh ginger minced
- 1 teaspoon fresh garlic minced
- 1 Tablespoon pure maple syrup

Directions for Cooking:
1) In a bowl, mix tofu with tamari and a tablespoon of cornstarch. Marinate for at least 15 minutes. Tossing well to coat every now and then.
2) In a small bowl mix all sauce Ingredients: and set aside.
3) Lightly grease baking pan of air fryer with cooking spray. Add tofu for 10 minutes, cook on 390°F. Halfway through cooking time, stir. Cook for 10 minutes more.
4) Stir in sauce, toss well to coat. Cook for another 5 minutes.
5) Serve and enjoy.

Nutrition Information:
Calories: 63; Carbs: 11.0g; Protein: 8.0g; Fat: 3.0g

Gouda-Spinach Stuffed Pork

(Servings: 2, Cooking Time: 15 minutes)

Ingredients:
- 3 tablespoons dry bread crumbs
- 2 tablespoons grated Parmesan cheese
- 2 pork sirloin cutlets (3 ounces each)
- 1/4 teaspoon salt
- 1/8 teaspoon pepper
- 2 slices smoked Gouda cheese (about 2 ounces)
- 2 cups fresh baby spinach
- 2 tablespoons horseradish mustard

Directions for Cooking:
1) Mix well Parmesan and bread crumbs in a small bowl.
2) On a flat surface, season pork with pepper and salt. Add spinach and cheese on each cutlet and fold to enclose filling. With toothpicks secure pork.
3) Brush mustard all over pork and dip in crumb mixture.
4) Lightly grease baking pan of air fryer with cooking spray. Add pork.
5) For 15 minutes, cook on 330°F. Halfway through cooking time, turnover.
6) Serve and enjoy.

Nutrition Information:
Calories: 304; Carbs: 10.0g; Protein: 30.0g; Fat: 16.0g

Scrumptious Shrimp Scampi Fry

(Servings: 4, Cooking Time: 15 minutes)

Ingredients:
- 4 tablespoons butter
- 1 tablespoon lemon juice
- 1 tablespoon minced garlic
- 2 teaspoons red pepper flakes
- 1 tablespoon chopped chives or 1 teaspoon dried chives
- 1 tablespoon minced basil leaves plus more for sprinkling or 1 teaspoon dried basil
- 2 tablespoons chicken stock (or white wine)
- 1-lb defrosted shrimp (21-25 count)

Directions for Cooking:
1) Lightly grease baking pan of air fryer with cooking spray. Melt butter for 2 minutes at 330°F. Stir in red pepper flakes and garlic. Cook for 3 minutes.
2) Add remaining Ingredients: in pan and toss well to coat.
3) Cook for 5 minutes at 330°F. Stir and let it stand for another 5 minutes.
4) Serve and enjoy.

Nutrition Information:
Calories: 213; Carbs: 1.0g; Protein: 23.0g; Fat: 13.0g

Baked Cod in Air Fryer

(Servings: 2, Cooking Time: 12 minutes)

Ingredients:
- 1 tablespoon butter
- 1/4 sleeve buttery round crackers (such as Ritz®), crushed
- 1 tablespoon butter
- 1/2 pound thick-cut cod loin
- 1/4 lemon, juiced
- 2 tablespoons dry white wine
- 1-1/2 teaspoons chopped fresh parsley
- 1-1/2 teaspoons chopped green onion
- 1/2 lemon, cut into wedges

Directions for Cooking:
1) In a small bowl, melt butter in microwave. Whisk in crackers.
2) Lightly grease baking pan of air fryer with remaining butter. And melt for 2 minutes at 390°F.
3) In a small bowl whisk well lemon juice, white wine, parsley, and green onion.
4) Coat cod filets in melted butter. Pour dressing. Top with butter-cracker mixture.
5) Cook for 10 minutes at 390°F.
6) Serve and enjoy with a slice of lemon.

Nutrition Information:
Calories: 266; Carbs: 9.3g; Protein: 20.9g; Fat: 16.1g

Tender Chicken Thigh Bake

(Servings: 4, Cooking Time: 11 minutes)

Ingredients:
- 4 bone-in chicken thighs with skin
- 1/8 teaspoon garlic salt
- 1/8 teaspoon onion salt
- 1/8 teaspoon dried oregano
- 1/8 teaspoon ground thyme
- 1/8 teaspoon paprika
- 1/8 teaspoon ground black pepper

Directions for Cooking:
1) Lightly grease baking pan of air fryer with cooking spray. Place chicken with skin side touching the bottom of pan.
2) In a small bowl whisk well pepper, paprika, thyme, oregano, onion salt, and garlic salt. Sprinkle all over chicken.
3) For 1 minute, cook on 390°F.
4) Turnover chicken while rubbing on bottom and sides of pan for more seasoning.
5) Cook for 10 minutes at 390°F.
6) Serve and enjoy.

Nutrition Information:
Calories: 185; Carbs: 0.2g; Protein: 19.2g; Fat: 11.9g

Chicken Teriyaki Bake

(Servings: 2, Cooking Time: 25 minutes)

Ingredients:
- 1-1/2 teaspoons cornstarch
- 1-1/2 teaspoons cold water
- 1/4 cup white sugar
- 1/4 cup soy sauce
- 2 tablespoons cider vinegar
- 1/2 clove garlic, minced
- 1/4 teaspoon ground ginger
- 1/8 teaspoon ground black pepper
- 4 skinless chicken thighs

Directions for Cooking:

1) Lightly grease baking pan of air fryer with cooking spray. Add all Ingredients: and toss well to coat. Spread chicken in a single layer on bottom of pan.
2) For 15 minutes, cook on 390°F.
3) Turnover chicken while brushing and covering well with the sauce.
4) Cook for 15 minutes at 330°F.
5) Serve and enjoy.

Nutrition Information:
Calories: 267; Carbs: 19.9g; Protein: 24.7g; Fat: 9.8g

Meatball Pizza Bake

(Servings: 4, Cooking Time: 15 minutes)

Ingredients:
- 1 prebaked 6-inch pizza crust
- 1/2 can (8 ounces) pizza sauce
- 1 teaspoon garlic powder
- 1 teaspoon Italian seasoning
- 4 tbsp grated Parmesan cheese
- 1 small onion, halved and sliced
- 6 frozen fully cooked Italian meatballs (1/2 ounce each), thawed and halved
- 1/2 cup shredded part-skim mozzarella cheese
- 1/2 cup shredded cheddar cheese

Directions for Cooking:

1) Lightly grease baking pan of air fryer with cooking spray.
2) Place crust on bottom of pan. Spread sauce on top. Sprinkle with parmesan, Italian seasoning, and garlic powder.
3) Top with meatballs and onion. Sprinkle remaining cheese.
4) For 15 minutes, cook on preheated 390°F air fryer.
5) Serve and enjoy.

Nutrition Information:
Calories: 324; Carbs: 28.0g; Protein: 17.0g; Fat: 16.0g

Pepperoni Calzone Bake

(Servings: 4, Cooking Time: 25 minutes)

Ingredients:
- 1 cup chopped pepperoni
- 1/2 cup pasta sauce with meat
- 1/4 cup shredded part-skim mozzarella cheese
- 1 loaf (1 pound) frozen bread dough, thawed
- 1 to 2 tablespoons 2% milk
- 1 tablespoon grated Parmesan cheese
- 1/2 teaspoon Italian seasoning, optional

Directions for Cooking:
1) In a bowl mix well mozzarella cheese, pizza sauce, and pepperoni.
2) On a lightly floured surface, divide dough into four portions. Roll each into a 6-in. circle; top each with a scant 1/3 cup pepperoni mixture. Fold dough over filling; pinch edges to seal.
3) Lightly grease baking pan of air fryer with cooking spray. Place dough in a single layer and if needed, cook in batches.
4) For 25 minutes, cook on 330°F preheated air fryer or until dough is lightly browned.
5) Serve and enjoy.

Nutrition Information:
Calories: 527; Carbs: 59.0g; Protein: 21.0g; Fat: 23.0g

Comforting Beef Stew Bake

(Servings: 4, Cooking Time: 40 minutes)

Ingredients:
- 1/2 can (14-1/2 ounces) diced tomatoes, undrained
- 1/2 cup water
- 2 tablespoons quick-cooking tapioca
- 1 teaspoon sugar
- 1 teaspoons salt
- 1/2 teaspoon pepper
- 1-pound beef stew meat, cut into 1-inch cubes
- 2 medium carrots, cut into 1-inch chunks
- 1 large potato, peeled and quartered
- 1 celery rib, cut into 3/4-inch chunks
- 1 small onion, cut into chunks
- 1 slice bread, cubed

Directions for Cooking:
1) Lightly grease baking pan of air fryer with cooking spray. Add all Ingredients: and toss well to coat.
2) Cover pan with foil.
3) For 25 minutes, cook on 390°F. Halfway through cooking time, stir.
4) Remove foil, stir well, and cook for 15 minutes at 330°F.
5) Serve and enjoy.

Nutrition Information:
Calories: 296; Carbs: 31.0g; Protein: 25.0g; Fat: 8.0g

Roll-up Chicken Reuben

(Servings: 2, Cooking Time: 15 minutes)

Ingredients:
- 2 slices swirled rye and pumpernickel bread
- 2 boneless skinless chicken breast halves (4 ounces each)
- 1/4 teaspoon garlic salt
- 1/4 teaspoon pepper
- 2 slices Swiss cheese
- 2 slices deli corned beef
- 2 tablespoons Thousand Island salad dressing
- Additional Thousand Island salad dressing, optional

Directions for Cooking:
1) Tear bread into 2-inch pieces and place in blender. Pulse until crumbly. Transfer to a shallow bowl.
2) With meal mallet, pound chicken to ¼*inch thick. Season with pepper and salt. Top chicken with corned beef and cheese. Roll chicken and secure ends with toothpick.
3) Brush chicken with dressing and dip in crumbs until covered totally.
4) Lightly grease baking pan of air fryer with cooking spray. Place rollups.
5) For 15 minutes, cook on 330°F preheated air fryer.
6) Turnover rollups and continue cooking for another 10 minutes.
7) Serve and enjoy with extra dressing.

Nutrition Information:
Calories: 317; Carbs: 18.0g; Protein: 32.0g; Fat: 13.0g

Chicken Mediterranean Fry

(Servings: 2, Cooking Time: 21 minutes)

Ingredients:
- 2 boneless skinless chicken breast halves (6 ounces each)
- 1/4 teaspoon salt
- 1/4 teaspoon pepper
- 3 tablespoons olive oil
- 1/2-pint grape tomatoes
- 6 pitted Greek or ripe olives, sliced
- 2 tablespoons capers, drained

Directions for Cooking:
1) Lightly grease baking pan of air fryer with cooking spray.
2) Add chicken and season with pepper and salt.
3) Brown for 3 minutes per side in preheated 390°F air fryer.
4) Stir in capers, olives, tomatoes, and oil.
5) Cook for 15 minutes at 330°F.
6) Serve and enjoy.

Nutrition Information:
Calories: 330; Carbs: 6.0g; Protein: 36.0g; Fat: 18.0g

Crusted Fish with Dijon

(Servings: 2, Cooking Time: 15 minutes)

Ingredients:
- 3 tablespoons reduced-fat mayonnaise
- 1 tablespoon lemon juice
- 2 teaspoons Dijon mustard
- 1 teaspoon prepared horseradish
- 2 tablespoons grated Parmesan cheese, divided
- 2 tilapia fillets (5 ounces each)
- 1/4 cup dry bread crumbs
- 2 teaspoons butter, melted

Directions for Cooking:

1) Lightly grease baking pan of air fryer with cooking spray. Place tilapia in a single layer.
2) In a small bowl, whisk well mayo, lemon juice, mustard, 1 tablespoon cheese and horseradish. Spread on top of fish.
3) In another bowl, mix remaining cheese, melted butter, and bread crumbs. Sprinkle on top of fish.
4) For 15 minutes, cook on 390°F.
5) Serve and enjoy.

Nutrition Information:
Calories: 212; Carbs: 7.0g; Protein: 28.0g; Fat: 8.0g

Rosemary Pork with Apricot Glaze

(Servings: 3, Cooking Time: 30 minutes)

Ingredients:
- 2 tablespoons minced fresh rosemary or 1 tablespoon dried rosemary, crushed
- 2 tablespoons olive oil, divided
- 4 garlic cloves, minced
- 1 teaspoon salt
- 1/2 teaspoon pepper
- 1-lb pork tenderloin

Apricot Glaze Ingredients:
- 1 cup apricot preserves
- 3 tablespoons lemon juice
- 2 garlic cloves, minced

Directions for Cooking:

1) Mix well pepper, salt, garlic, oil, and rosemary. Brush all over pork. If needed cut pork crosswise in half to fit in air fryer.
2) Lightly grease baking pan of air fryer with cooking spray. Add pork.
3) For 3 minutes per side, brown pork in a preheated 390°F air fryer.
4) Meanwhile, mix well all glaze Ingredients: in a small bowl. Baste pork every 5 minutes.
5) Cook for 20 minutes at 330°F.
6) Serve and enjoy.

Nutrition Information:
Calories: 281; Carbs: 27.0g; Protein: 23.0g; Fat: 9.0g

Creamy Coconut Sauce on Jamaican Salmon

(Servings: 2, Cooking Time: 12 minutes)

Ingredients:
- 2 salmon fillets (6 ounces each)
- 1 ½ tablespoons mayonnaise
- 2 teaspoons Caribbean jerk seasoning
- 1/4 cup sour cream
- 4 tbsp cream of coconut
- 1 teaspoon grated lime zest
- 4 tbsp cup lime juice
- 1/4 cup sweetened shredded coconut, toasted

Directions for Cooking:
1) Lightly grease baking pan of air fryer with cooking spray. Add salmon with skin side down. Spread mayo on top and season with Caribbean jerk.
2) For 12 minutes, cook on 330°F.
3) On medium low fire, place a pan and bring lime juice, lime zest, cream of coconut, and sour cream to a simmer. Mix well. Transfer to a bowl for dipping.
4) Serve and enjoy.

Nutrition Information:
Calories: 490; Carbs: 16.0g; Protein: 30.0g; Fat: 34.0g

Turkey 'n Biscuit Bake

(Servings: 5, Cooking Time: 30 minutes)

Ingredients:
- 1 can (10-3/4 ounces) condensed cream of chicken soup, undiluted
- 1 cup chopped cooked turkey or chicken
- 1 can (4 ounces) mushroom stems and pieces, drained
- 1/2 cup frozen peas
- 1/4 cup 2% milk
- Dash each ground cumin, dried basil and thyme
- 1 tube (12 ounces) refrigerated buttermilk biscuits, cut into 4 equal slices

Directions for Cooking:
1) Lightly grease baking pan of air fryer with cooking spray. Add all Ingredients: and toss well to mix except for biscuits.
2) Top with biscuits. Cover pan with foil.
3) For 15 minutes, cook on 390°F.
4) Remove foil and cook for 15 minutes at 330°F or until biscuits are lightly browned.
5) Serve and enjoy.

Nutrition Information:
Calories: 325; Carbs: 38.0g; Protein: 14.0g; Fat: 13.0g

Chicken Bruschetta Bake

(Servings: 2, Cooking Time: 28 minutes)

Ingredients:
- 1/4 cup all-purpose flour
- 1/4 cup egg substitute
- 2 boneless skinless chicken breast halves (4 ounces each)
- 1/4 cup grated Parmesan cheese
- 1/4 cup dry bread crumbs
- 1 tablespoon butter, melted
- 1 large tomato, seeded and chopped
- 1 1/2 tablespoons minced fresh basil
- 1/2 tablespoon olive oil
- 2 garlic cloves, minced
- 1/2 teaspoon salt
- 1/4 teaspoon pepper

Directions for Cooking:
1) In shallow bowl, whisk well egg substitute and place flour in a separate bowl. Dip chicken in flour, then egg, and then flour. In small bowl whisk well butter, bread crumbs and cheese. Sprinkle over chicken.
2) Lightly grease baking pan of air fryer with cooking spray. Place breaded chicken on bottom of pan. Cover with foil.
3) For 20 minutes, cook on 390°F.
4) Meanwhile, in a bowl whisk well remaining ingredient.
5) Remove foil from pan and then pour over chicken the remaining Ingredients.
6) Cook for 8 minutes.
7) Serve and enjoy.

Nutrition Information:
Calories: 311; Carbs: 22.0g; Protein: 31.0g; Fat: 11.0g

Amazingly Healthy Zucchini Bake

(Servings: 5, Cooking Time: 20 minutes)

Ingredients:
- 1 large zucchini, cut lengthwise then in half
- 1 (8 ounce) package cream cheese, softened
- 1 cup sour cream
- 1/4 cup grated Parmesan cheese
- 1 tablespoon minced garlic
- paprika to taste

Directions for Cooking:
1) Lightly grease baking pan of air fryer with cooking spray.
2) Place zucchini slices in a single layer in pan.
3) In a bowl whisk well, remaining Ingredients: except for paprika. Spread on top of zucchini slices. Sprinkle paprika.
4) Cover pan with foil.
5) For 10 minutes, cook on 390°F.
6) Remove foil and cook for 10 minutes at 330°F.
7) Serve and enjoy.

Nutrition Information:
Calories: 296; Carbs: 6.5g; Protein: 7.3g; Fat: 26.7g

3-Cheese Meatball Bake

(Servings: 5, Cooking Time: 40 minutes)

Ingredients:
- 1/2 package (16 ounces) mostaccioli, cooked according to package Directions for Cooking: and drained
- 1 large Egg, lightly beaten
- 1/2 carton (15 ounces) part-skim ricotta cheese
- 1/2-pound ground beef
- 1 small onion, chopped
- 1 tablespoon brown sugar
- 1 tablespoon Italian seasoning
- 1 teaspoon garlic powder
- 1/4 teaspoon pepper
- 1 jar (24 ounces) pasta sauce with meat
- 1/4 cup grated Romano cheese
- 1/2 package (12 ounces) frozen fully cooked Italian meatballs, thawed
- 1/4 cup shaved Parmesan cheese
- Minced fresh parsley or fresh baby arugula, optional

Directions for Cooking:
1) Lightly grease baking pan of air fryer with cooking spray. Add beef and onions.
2) Cook for 10 minutes at 330°F, stirring and crumbling halfway through cooking time.
3) Drain excess fat. Stir in sugar and seasoning.
4) Mix in pasta and sauce. Mix well.
5) Remove half of mixture and transfer to a plate. Evenly spread half of ricotta mixture and half of Romano cheese. Return half of pasta. Evenly spread remaining ricotta and Romano. Top with meatballs and Parmesan.
6) Cover with foil.
7) For 20 minutes, cook on 390°F.
8) Remove foil cook for 10 minutes more until tops are lightly browned.
9) Serve and enjoy.

Nutrition Information:
Calories: 563; Carbs: 55.0g; Protein: 34.0g; Fat: 23.0g

Tater Tot, Cheeseburger 'n Bacon Bake

(Servings: 6, Cooking Time: 35 minutes)

Ingredients:
- 1-pound ground beef
- 1 small onion, chopped
- 1/2 can (15 ounces) tomato sauce
- 4-ounces process cheese (Velveeta)
- 1 tablespoon ground mustard
- 1 tablespoon Worcestershire sauce
- 1/2 cup shredded cheddar cheese
- 6 bacon strips, cooked and crumbled
- 8-ounces frozen Tater Tots
- 1/2 cup grape tomatoes, chopped
- 1/4 cup sliced dill pickles

Directions for Cooking:
1) Lightly grease baking pan of air fryer with cooking spray. Add beef and half of onions.
2) For 10 minutes, cook on 390°F. Halfway through cooking time, stir and crumble beef.
3) Stir in Worcestershire, mustard, Velveeta, and tomato sauce. Mix well. Cook for 4 minutes until melted.

4) Mix well and evenly spread in pan. Top with cheddar cheese and then bacon strips.
5) Evenly top with tater tots. Cover pan with foil.
6) Cook for 15 minutes at 390°F. Uncover and bake for 10 minutes more until tops are lightly browned.
7) Serve and enjoy topped with pickles and tomatoes and remaining onion.

Nutrition Information:
Calories: 483; Carbs: 24.0g; Protein: 27.0g; Fat: 31.0g

Chicago-Style Deep Dish Pizza

(Servings: 4, Cooking Time: 25 minutes)

Ingredients:
- 1 package (1/4 ounce) active dry yeast
- 1 cup warm water (110°F to 115°F)
- 1 teaspoon sugar
- 1 teaspoon salt
- 2 tablespoons canola oil
- 2-1/2 cups all-purpose flour
- 1-pound ground beef, cooked and drained
- 1 can (10-3/4 ounces) condensed tomato soup, undiluted
- 1 teaspoon each dried basil, oregano and thyme
- 1 teaspoon dried rosemary, crushed
- 1/4 teaspoon garlic powder
- 1 small green pepper, julienned
- 1 can (8 ounces) mushroom stems and pieces, drained
- 1 cup shredded part-skim mozzarella cheese

Directions for Cooking:

1) In a large bowl, dissolve yeast in warm water. Add the sugar, salt, oil and 2 cups flour. Beat until smooth. Stir in enough remaining flour to form a soft dough. Cover and let rest for 20 minutes. Divide into two and store half in the freezer for future use.
2) On a floured surface, roll into a square the size of your air fryer. Transfer to a greased air fryer baking pan. Sprinkle with beef.
3) Mix well seasonings and soup in a small bowl and pour over beef.
4) Sprinkle top with mushrooms and green pepper. Top with cheese.
5) Cover pan with foil.
6) For 15 minutes, cook on 390°F.
7) Remove foil, cook for another 10 minutes or until cheese is melted.
8) Serve and enjoy.

Nutrition Information:
Calories: 362; Carbs: 39.0g; Protein: 20.0g; Fat: 14.0g

1000 Days Air Fryer Meal Plan

1st day	2nd day	3rd day	4th day	5th day	6th day	7th day	8th day	9th day	10th day
Creamy Broccoli Egg Scramble	Veggie-Pasta 'n chicken Bake	Eggplant-Parm Bake	Butterflied Chicken with Herbs	Air Fried Grilled Asparagus	Grilled Sweet Potato Wedges with Dipping Sauce	Roasted Tuna on Linguine	Grilled BBQ Sausages	Appealingly Coconut-y Cake	Hungarian Style Grilled Beef
11th day	12th day	13th day	14th day	15th day	16th day	17th day	18th day	19th day	20th day
Loaded Breakfast Hash Browns	Penne Chicken Pesto Bake	Seven Layers of Tortilla Pie	4-Ingredient Garlic Herb Chicken Wings	Grilled Hasselback Potatoes	Grilled Green Beans with Shallots	Chili Lime Clams with Tomatoes	Medium Rare Simple Salt and Pepper Steak	Beef Eastern Shish Kebabs	Orange & Tofu Fry
21st day	22nd day	23rd day	24th day	25th day	26th day	27th day	28th day	29th day	30th day
Biscuit, Sausage 'n Egg Layer Casserole	Chicken Florentine Bake	Penne Pasta 'n Portobello Bake	Pesto Grilled Chicken	Air Fryer Roasted Vegetables	Grille Tomatoes with Garden Herb Salad	Air Fryer Garlicky-Grilled Turbot	Pounded Flank Steak with Tomato Salsa	Grilled Chicken Shish Tanoak	Scrumptious Shrimp Scampi Fry
31st day	32nd day	33rd day	34th day	35th day	36th day	37th day	38th day	39th day	40th day
Easy Italian Frittata	Cheesy Broccoli-Rice Bake	Feta-Spinach 'n Pita Casserole	Chili and Yogurt Marinated Chicken	Air Fried Roasted Summer Squash	Grilled Potato Packets	Broiled Spiced-Lemon Squid	Strip Steak with Japanese Dipping Sauce	Sweetly Honeyed Chicken Kebabs	Salmon with Crisped Topped Crumbs
41st day	42nd day	43rd day	44th day	45th day	46th day	47th day	48th day	49th day	50th day
Breakfast Biscuits, Eggs 'n Bacon	Green Bean ' Chicken Stuffing Bake	Southwest Style Meaty Casserole	Grilled Chicken with Board Dressing	Grilled Cauliflower Bites	Grilled Sweet Onions	Tuna Grill with Ginger Sauce	Chi Spacca's Bistecca	Chicken and Pineapple BBQ	Baked Cod in Air Fryer
51st day	52nd day	53rd day	54th day	55th day	56th day	57th day	58th day	59th day	60th day
Hash Brown, Sausage 'n Cauliflower Bake	Yummy Mac 'n Cheese	Nutritious Cabbage Roll Bake	Indian Spiced Chicken Eggplant and Tomato Skewers	Roasted Air Fried Vegetables	Roasted Dill Potato Medley	Char-Grilled Spicy Halibut	Grilled Steak with Parsley Salad	Skewered Beef Asian Way	Orange-Caesar Dressed Roughie
61st day	62nd day	63rd day	64th day	65th day	66th day	67th day	68th day	69th day	70th day
Cauliflower-Broccoli Egg Bake	Mouth-Watering Taco Bake	Easy-Bake Spanish Rice	Easy Curry Grilled Chicken Wings	Air Fryer Grilled Mexican Corn	Grilled Squash	Roasted Swordfish with Charred Leeks	Korean Grilled Skirt Steak	Chicken Kebabs Greek Way	Gouda-Spinach Stuffed Pork

71st day	72nd day	73rd day	74th day	75th day	76th day	77th day	78th day	79th day	80th day
Raisin 'n Apple French Toast	Rice Casserole Mexican Style	Brown Rice 'n Chicken Curry Casserole	Spicy Chicken with Lemon and Parsley in A Packet	Crispy and Spicy Grilled Broccoli in Air Fryer	Air Fryer Grilled Fennel	Citrusy Branzini on the Grill	Onion Marinated Skirt Steak	Skewered Oriental Teriyaki Beef	Buffalo Chicken Dip Bake
81st day	82nd day	83rd day	84th day	85th day	86th day	87th day	88th day	89th day	90th day
Overnight French Toast with Blueberries	Black Bean and Brown Rice Bake	Rotisserie Chicken with Herbes De Provence	Korean Grilled Chicken	Easy Grilled Corn in The Air Fryer	Grilled Corn Kabobs	Grilled Squid Rings with Kale and Tomatoes	Grilled Beef Steak with Herby Marinade	Grilled Beef with Ginger-Hoisin	Tender Chicken Thigh Bake
91st day	92nd day	93rd day	94th day	95th day	96th day	97th day	98th day	99th day	100th day
Eggs Benedict in an Overnight Casserole	Herb and Zucchini Bake	Grilled Oregano Chicken	Grilled Chicken with Shishito Peppers	Grilled Pineapple and Peppers	Grill Smoked Mushrooms	Butterflied Sriracha Prawns Grilled	Crunchy Crisped Peaches	Spiced Lime 'n Coconut Shrimp Skewer	Chicken Teriyaki Bake
101st day	102nd day	103rd day	104th day	105th day	106th day	107th day	108th day	109th day	110th day
Egg-Substitute 'n Bacon Casserole	A Different Rice-Chik'n Bake	Honey Sriracha Chicken	Grilled Chicken with Scallions	Grilled Onion Potatoes	Blackened Shrimps in Air Fryer	Grilled Shrimp with Butter	Five-Cheese Pull Apart Bread	Teriyaki 'n Hawaiian Chicken	Meatball Pizza Bake
111th day	112th day	113th day	114th day	115th day	116th day	117th day	118th day	119th day	120th day
Country style Brekky Casserole	Sea Scallop Bake	Tequila Glazed Chicken	Piri Piri Chicken	Grilled Frozen Vegetables	Herb and Garlic Fish Fingers	Char-Grilled 'n Herbed Sea Scallops	Buttery Dinner Rolls	Tangy Grilled Fig-Prosciutto	Pepperoni Calzone Bake
121st day	122nd day	123rd day	124th day	125th day	126th day	127th day	128th day	129th day	130th day
Amish Style Brekky Casserole	Portuguese Bacalao Tapas	Grilled Sambal Chicken	Grilled Turmeric and Lemongrass Chicken	Simple Grilled Vegetables	Crispy Cod Nuggets with Tartar Sauce	Japanese Citrus Soy Squid	Yummy Carrot Cake	Veggie Souvlaki on Air Fryer Grill	Comforting Beef Stew Bake
131st day	132nd day	133rd day	134th day	135th day	136th day	137th day	138th day	139th day	140th day
Baked Cornbread and Eggs	Shrimp Casserole Louisiana Style	Smoked Chicken Wings	Peruvian Grilled Chicken	Italian Grilled Vegetables	Garlic and Black Pepper Shrimp Grill	Greek-Style Grilled Scallops	Tangy Orange-Chococake	Swordfish with Sage on the Grill	Roll-up Chicken Reuben
141st day	142nd day	143rd day	144th day	145th day	146th day	147th day	148th day	149th day	150th day

Feta and Spinach Brekky Pie	Lobster Lasagna Maine Style	Sweet and Sour Grilled Chicken	Air Fryer Grilled Moroccan Chicken	Balsamic Grilled Vegetables	Grilled Salmon with Cucumbers	Easy Grilled Pesto Scallops	Delightful Caramel Cheesecake	Scallops and Bacon Grill	Chicken Mediterranean Fry
151st day	152nd day	153rd day	154th day	155th day	156th day	157th day	158th day	159th day	160th day
Cheesy-Bacon Casserole	Rice and Tuna Puff	Lemon Grilled Chicken Breasts	Rotisserie Chicken with Herbes De Provence	Grilled Vegetables with Lemon Herb Vinaigrette	Shrimps, Zucchini, And Tomatoes on the Grill	Clams with Herbed Butter in Packets	Amazing with Every Bite Fried Bananas	Grilled Chipotle Shrimp	3-Cheese Meatball Bake
161st day	162nd day	163rd day	164th day	165th day	166th day	167th day	168th day	169th day	170th day
Mixed Vegetable Frittata	Cheesy Zucchini-Squash Bake	Spicy Peach Glazed Grilled Chicken	Grilled Oregano Chicken	Grilled Vegetables with Garlic	Grilled Halibut with Tomatoes and Hearts of Palm	Simple Sesame Squid on the Grill	Sugared Doughs with Choco Dip	Dill-Rubbed Grilled Salmon	Crusted Fish with Dijon
171st day	172nd day	173rd day	174th day	175th day	176th day	177th day	178th day	179th day	180th day
Breakfast Chicken Casserole	Yellow Squash Bake, Low Carb	Chinese Style Chicken	Honey Sriracha Chicken	Grilled Asparagus with Hollandaise Sauce	Chat Masala Grilled Snapper	Grilled Shellfish with Vegetables	Enchanting Coffee-Apple Cake	Turkey Meatballs in Skewer	Rosemary Pork with Apricot Glaze
181st day	182nd day	183rd day	184th day	185th day	186th day	187th day	188th day	189th day	190th day
Rice Casserole Mexican Style	Zucchini & Carrot Bake	Garlic Cilantro-Lime Chicken	Tequila Glazed Chicken	Grilled Zucchini with Mozzarella	One-Pan Shrimp and Chorizo Mix Grill	Grilled Meat Recipes	Pumpkin Pie in Air Fryer	Grilled Curried Chicken	Tater Tot, Cheeseburger 'n Bacon Bake
191st day	192nd day	193rd day	194th day	195th day	196th day	197th day	198th day	199th day	200th day
Broccoli, Ham 'n Potato Casserole	Cheesy-Creamy Broccoli Bake	Grilled Chicken Stuffed with Cheese	Grilled Sambal Chicken	Grilled Tomato Melts	Grilled Tasty Scallops	Sous Vide Smoked Brisket	Blackberry-Goodness Cobbler	Chicken Caesar on the Grill	Chicago-Style Deep Dish Pizza
201st day	202nd day	203rd day	204th day	205th day	206th day	207th day	208th day	209th day	210th day
Cheeseburger and Bacon Casserole	Mushroom 'n Spinach Casserole	Southwest Chicken Foil Packets	Smoked Chicken Wings	Grilled Asparagus and Arugula Salad	Clam with Lemons on the Grill	Skirt Steak with Mojo Marinade	Appetizing Apple Pound Cake	Grilled Jerk Chicken	Creamy Coconut Sauce on Jamaican Salmon
211th day	212th day	213th day	214th day	215th day	216th day	217th day	218th day	219th day	220th day

Vegan Approved Shepherd's Pie	Potato Casserole Twice Baked	Teriyaki Grilled Chicken	Sweet and Sour Grilled Chicken	Air Fryer Grilled Mushrooms	Salmon Steak Grilled with Cilantro Garlic Sauce	Dijon-Marinated Skirt Steak	Cranberry Bread Pudding	Rosemary-Rubbed Grilled Lamb	Chicken Bruschetta Bake
221st day	**222nd day**	**223rd day**	**224th day**	**225th day**	**226th day**	**227th day**	**228th day**	**229th day**	**230th day**
Enchilada Leftovers Casserole	Chicken Deluxe Tetrazzini	Sweet and Spicy Grilled Chicken	Lemon Grilled Chicken Breasts	Spicy Thai – Style Veggies	Tasty Grilled Red Mullet	Grilled Carne Asada Steak	Easy 'n Delicious Brownies	Thai-Style Grilled Pork	Turkey 'n Biscuit Bake
231st day	**232nd day**	**233rd day**	**234th day**	**235th day**	**236th day**	**237th day**	**238th day**	**239th day**	**240th day**
Rice, Chicken 'n Salsa Casserole	Chili Rellenos Bake	Hone, Lime, And Lime Grilled Chicken	Spicy Peach Glazed Grilled Chicken	Grilled Vegetables with Smokey Mustard Sauce	Chargrilled Halibut Niçoise With Vegetables	Chimichurri-Style Steak	Luscious Strawberry Cobbler	Cajun Pork on the Grill	Amazingly Healthy Zucchini Bake
241st day	**242nd day**	**243rd day**	**244th day**	**245th day**	**246th day**	**247th day**	**248th day**	**249th day**	**250th day**
Turkey 'n Broccoli Bake	Spicy Zucchini Bake Mexican Style	Grilled Jerk Chicken	Chinese Style Chicken	Indian Grilled Vegetables	Spiced Salmon Kebabs	Strip Steak with Cucumber Yogurt Sauce	Sour Cream-Blueberry Coffee Cake	Grilled Buccaneer Pork	Grilled Frozen Vegetables
251st day	**252nd day**	**253rd day**	**254th day**	**255th day**	**256th day**	**257th day**	**258th day**	**259th day**	**260th day**
Creamy Broccoli Egg Scramble	Veggie-Pasta 'n chicken Bake	Eggplant-Parm Bake	Butterflied Chicken with Herbs	Air Fried Grilled Asparagus	Grilled Sweet Potato Wedges with Dipping Sauce	Roasted Tuna on Linguine	Grilled BBQ Sausages	Appealingly Coconut-y Cake	Hungarian Style Grilled Beef
261st day	**262nd day**	**263rd day**	**264th day**	**265th day**	**266th day**	**267th day**	**268th day**	**269th day**	**270th day**
Loaded Breakfast Hash Browns	Penne Chicken Pesto Bake	Seven Layers of Tortilla Pie	4-Ingredient Garlic Herb Chicken Wings	Grilled Hasselback Potatoes	Grilled Green Beans with Shallots	Chili Lime Clams with Tomatoes	Medium Rare Simple Salt and Pepper Steak	Beef Eastern Shish Kebabs	Orange & Tofu Fry
271st day	**272nd day**	**273rd day**	**274th day**	**275th day**	**276th day**	**277th day**	**278th day**	**279th day**	**280th day**
Biscuit, Sausage 'n Egg Layer Casserole	Chicken Florentine Bake	Penne Pasta 'n Portobello Bake	Pesto Grilled Chicken	Air Fryer Roasted Vegetables	Grille Tomatoes with Garden Herb Salad	Air Fryer Garlicky-Grilled Turbot	Pounded Flank Steak with Tomato Salsa	Grilled Chicken Shish Tanoak	Scrumptious Shrimp Scampi Fry
281st day	**282nd day**	**283rd day**	**284th day**	**285th day**	**286th day**	**287th day**	**288th day**	**289th day**	**290th day**

Easy Italian Frittata	Cheesy Broccoli-Rice Bake	Feta-Spinach 'n Pita Casserole	Chili and Yogurt Marinated Chicken	Air Fried Roasted Summer Squash	Grilled Potato Packets	Broiled Spiced-Lemon Squid	Strip Steak with Japanese Dipping Sauce	Sweetly Honeyed Chicken Kebabs	Salmon with Crisped Topped Crumbs
291st day	292nd day	293rd day	294th day	295th day	296th day	297th day	298th day	299th day	300th day
Breakfast Biscuits, Eggs 'n Bacon	Green Bean 'Chicken Stuffing Bake	Southwest Style Meaty Casserole	Grilled Chicken with Board Dressing	Grilled Cauliflower Bites	Grilled Sweet Onions	Tuna Grill with Ginger Sauce	Chi Spacca's Bistecca	Chicken and Pineapple BBQ	Baked Cod in Air Fryer
301st day	302nd day	303rd day	304th day	305th day	306th day	307th day	308th day	309th day	310th day
Hash Brown, Sausage 'n Cauliflower Bake	Yummy Mac 'n Cheese	Nutritious Cabbage Roll Bake	Indian Spiced Chicken Eggplant and Tomato Skewers	Roasted Air Fried Vegetables	Roasted Dill Potato Medley	Char-Grilled Spicy Halibut	Grilled Steak with Parsley Salad	Skewered Beef Asian Way	Orange-Caesar Dressed Roughie
311th day	312th day	313th day	314th day	315th day	316th day	317th day	318th day	319th day	320th day
Cauliflower-Broccoli Egg Bake	Mouth-Watering Taco Bake	Easy-Bake Spanish Rice	Easy Curry Grilled Chicken Wings	Air Fryer Grilled Mexican Corn	Grilled Squash	Roasted Swordfish with Charred Leeks	Korean Grilled Skirt Steak	Chicken Kebabs Greek Way	Gouda-Spinach Stuffed Pork
321st day	322nd day	323rd day	324th day	325th day	326th day	327th day	328th day	329th day	330th day
Raisin 'n Apple French Toast	Rice Casserole Mexican Style	Brown Rice 'n Chicken Curry Casserole	Spicy Chicken with Lemon and Parsley in A Packet	Crispy and Spicy Grilled Broccoli in Air Fryer	Air Fryer Grilled Fennel	Citrusy Branzini on the Grill	Onion Marinated Skirt Steak	Skewered Oriental Teriyaki Beef	Buffalo Chicken Dip Bake
331st day	332nd day	333rd day	334th day	335th day	336th day	337th day	338th day	339th day	340th day
Overnight French Toast with Blueberries	Black Bean and Brown Rice Bake	Rotisserie Chicken with Herbes De Provence	Korean Grilled Chicken	Easy Grilled Corn in The Air Fryer	Grilled Corn Kabobs	Grilled Squid Rings with Kale and Tomatoes	Grilled Beef Steak with Herby Marinade	Grilled Beef with Ginger-Hoisin	Tender Chicken Thigh Bake
341st day	342nd day	343rd day	344th day	345th day	346th day	347th day	348th day	349th day	350th day
Eggs Benedict in an Overnight Casserole	Herb and Zucchini Bake	Grilled Oregano Chicken	Grilled Chicken with Shishito Peppers	Grilled Pineapple and Peppers	Grill Smoked Mushrooms	Butterflied Sriracha Prawns Grilled	Crunchy Crisped Peaches	Spiced Lime 'n Coconut Shrimp Skewer	Chicken Teriyaki Bake
351st day	352nd day	353rd day	354th day	355th day	356th day	357th day	358th day	359th day	360th day

142

Egg-Substitute 'n Bacon Casserole	A Different Rice-Chik'n Bake	Honey Sriracha Chicken	Grilled Chicken with Scallions	Grilled Onion Potatoes	Blackened Shrimps in Air Fryer	Grilled Shrimp with Butter	Five-Cheese Pull Apart Bread	Teriyaki 'n Hawaiian Chicken	Meatball Pizza Bake
361st day	**362nd day**	**363rd day**	**364th day**	**365th day**	**366th day**	**367th day**	**368th day**	**369th day**	**370th day**
Country style Brekky Casserole	Sea Scallop Bake	Tequila Glazed Chicken	Piri Piri Chicken	Grilled Frozen Vegetables	Herb and Garlic Fish Fingers	Char-Grilled 'n Herbed Sea Scallops	Buttery Dinner Rolls	Tangy Grilled Fig-Prosciutto	Pepperoni Calzone Bake
371st day	**372nd day**	**373rd day**	**374th day**	**375th day**	**376th day**	**377th day**	**378th day**	**379th day**	**380th day**
Amish Style Brekky Casserole	Portuguese Bacalao Tapas	Grilled Sambal Chicken	Grilled Turmeric and Lemongrass Chicken	Simple Grilled Vegetables	Crispy Cod Nuggets with Tartar Sauce	Japanese Citrus Soy Squid	Yummy Carrot Cake	Veggie Souvlaki on Air Fryer Grill	Comforting Beef Stew Bake
381st day	**382nd day**	**383rd day**	**384th day**	**385th day**	**386th day**	**387th day**	**388th day**	**389th day**	**390th day**
Baked Cornbread and Eggs	Shrimp Casserole Louisiana Style	Smoked Chicken Wings	Peruvian Grilled Chicken	Italian Grilled Vegetables	Garlic and Black Pepper Shrimp Grill	Greek-Style Grilled Scallops	Tangy Orange-Choco cake	Swordfish with Sage on the Grill	Roll-up Chicken Reuben
391st day	**392nd day**	**393rd day**	**394th day**	**395th day**	**396th day**	**397th day**	**398th day**	**399th day**	**400th day**
Feta and Spinach Brekky Pie	Lobster Lasagna Maine Style	Sweet and Sour Grilled Chicken	Air Fryer Grilled Moroccan Chicken	Balsamic Grilled Vegetables	Grilled Salmon with Cucumbers	Easy Grilled Pesto Scallops	Delightful Caramel Cheesecake	Scallops and Bacon Grill	Chicken Mediterranean Fry
401st day	**402nd day**	**403rd day**	**404th day**	**405th day**	**406th day**	**407th day**	**408th day**	**409th day**	**410th day**
Cheesy-Bacon Casserole	Rice and Tuna Puff	Lemon Grilled Chicken Breasts	Rotisserie Chicken with Herbes De Provence	Grilled Vegetables with Lemon Herb Vinaigrette	Shrimps, Zucchini, And Tomatoes on the Grill	Clams with Herbed Butter in Packets	Amazing with Every Bite Fried Bananas	Grilled Chipotle Shrimp	3-Cheese Meatball Bake
411th day	**412th day**	**413th day**	**414th day**	**415th day**	**416th day**	**417th day**	**418th day**	**419th day**	**420th day**
Mixed Vegetable Frittata	Cheesy Zucchini-Squash Bake	Spicy Peach Glazed Grilled Chicken	Grilled Oregano Chicken	Grilled Vegetables with Garlic	Grilled Halibut with Tomatoes and Hearts of Palm	Simple Sesame Squid on the Grill	Sugared Doughs with Choco Dip	Dill-Rubbed Grilled Salmon	Crusted Fish with Dijon
421st day	**422nd day**	**423rd day**	**424th day**	**425th day**	**426th day**	**427th day**	**428th day**	**429th day**	**430th day**
Breakfast Chicken Casserole	Yellow Squash Bake, Low Carb	Chinese Style Chicken	Honey Sriracha Chicken	Grilled Asparagus with Holland	Chat Masala Grilled Snapper	Grilled Shellfish with Vegetables	Enchanting Coffee-Apple Cake	Turkey Meatballs in Skewer	Rosemary Pork with Apricot Glaze

				aise Sauce					
431st day	**432nd day**	**433rd day**	**434th day**	**435th day**	**436th day**	**437th day**	**438th day**	**439th day**	**440th day**
Rice Casserole Mexican Style	Zucchini & Carrot Bake	Garlic Cilantro-Lime Chicken	Tequila Glazed Chicken	Grilled Zucchini with Mozzarella	One-Pan Shrimp and Chorizo Mix Grill	Grilled Meat Recipes	Pumpkin Pie in Air Fryer	Grilled Curried Chicken	Tater Tot, Cheeseburger 'n Bacon Bake
441st day	**442nd day**	**443rd day**	**444th day**	**445th day**	**446th day**	**447th day**	**448th day**	**449th day**	**450th day**
Broccoli, Ham 'n Potato Casserole	Cheesy-Creamy Broccoli Bake	Grilled Chicken Stuffed with Cheese	Grilled Sambal Chicken	Grilled Tomato Melts	Grilled Tasty Scallops	Sous Vide Smoked Brisket	Blackberry-Goodness Cobbler	Chicken Caesar on the Grill	Chicago-Style Deep Dish Pizza
451st day	**452nd day**	**453rd day**	**454th day**	**455th day**	**456th day**	**457th day**	**458th day**	**459th day**	**460th day**
Cheeseburger and Bacon Casserole	Mushroom 'n Spinach Casserole	Southwest Chicken Foil Packets	Smoked Chicken Wings	Grilled Asparagus and Arugula Salad	Clam with Lemons on the Grill	Skirt Steak with Mojo Marinade	Appetizing Apple Pound Cake	Grilled Jerk Chicken	Creamy Coconut Sauce on Jamaican Salmon
461st day	**462nd day**	**463rd day**	**464th day**	**465th day**	**466th day**	**467th day**	**468th day**	**469th day**	**470th day**
Vegan Approved Shepherd's Pie	Potato Casserole Twice Baked	Teriyaki Grilled Chicken	Sweet and Sour Grilled Chicken	Air Fryer Grilled Mushrooms	Salmon Steak Grilled with Cilantro Garlic Sauce	Dijon-Marinated Skirt Steak	Cranberry Bread Pudding	Rosemary-Rubbed Grilled Lamb	Chicken Bruschetta Bake
471st day	**472nd day**	**473rd day**	**474th day**	**475th day**	**476th day**	**477th day**	**478th day**	**479th day**	**480th day**
Enchilada Leftovers Casserole	Chicken Deluxe Tetrazzini	Sweet and Spicy Grilled Chicken	Lemon Grilled Chicken Breasts	Spicy Thai – Style Veggies	Tasty Grilled Red Mullet	Grilled Carne Asada Steak	Easy 'n Delicious Brownies	Thai-Style Grilled Pork	Turkey 'n Biscuit Bake
481st day	**482nd day**	**483rd day**	**484th day**	**485th day**	**486th day**	**487th day**	**488th day**	**489th day**	**490th day**
Rice, Chicken 'n Salsa Casserole	Chili Rellenos Bake	Hone, Lime, And Lime Grilled Chicken	Spicy Peach Glazed Grilled Chicken	Grilled Vegetables with Smokey Mustard Sauce	Chargrilled Halibut Niçoise With Vegetables	Chimichurri-Style Steak	Luscious Strawberry Cobbler	Cajun Pork on the Grill	Amazingly Healthy Zucchini Bake
491st day	**492nd day**	**493rd day**	**494th day**	**495th day**	**496th day**	**497th day**	**498th day**	**499th day**	**500th day**
Turkey 'n Broccoli Bake	Spicy Zucchini Bake Mexican Style	Grilled Jerk Chicken	Chinese Style Chicken	Indian Grilled Vegetables	Spiced Salmon Kebabs	Strip Steak with Cucumb	Sour Cream-Blueberry	Grilled Buccaneer Pork	Grilled Frozen Vegetables

						er Yogurt Sauce	Coffee Cake		
501st day	**502nd day**	**503rd day**	**504th day**	**505th day**	**506th day**	**507th day**	**508th day**	**509th day**	**510th day**
Creamy Broccoli Egg Scramble	Veggie-Pasta 'n chicken Bake	Eggplant-Parm Bake	Butterflied Chicken with Herbs	Air Fried Grilled Asparagus	Grilled Sweet Potato Wedges with Dipping Sauce	Roasted Tuna on Linguine	Grilled BBQ Sausages	Appealingly Coconut-y Cake	Hungarian Style Grilled Beef
511th day	**512th day**	**513th day**	**514th day**	**515th day**	**516th day**	**517th day**	**518th day**	**519th day**	**520th day**
Loaded Breakfast Hash Browns	Penne Chicken Pesto Bake	Seven Layers of Tortilla Pie	4-Ingredient Garlic Herb Chicken Wings	Grilled Hasselback Potatoes	Grilled Green Beans with Shallots	Chili Lime Clams with Tomatoes	Medium Rare Simple Salt and Pepper Steak	Beef Eastern Shish Kebabs	Orange & Tofu Fry
521st day	**522nd day**	**523rd day**	**524th day**	**525th day**	**526th day**	**527th day**	**528th day**	**529th day**	**530th day**
Biscuit, Sausage 'n Egg Layer Casserole	Chicken Florentine Bake	Penne Pasta 'n Portobello Bake	Pesto Grilled Chicken	Air Fryer Roasted Vegetables	Grille Tomatoes with Garden Herb Salad	Air Fryer Garlicky-Grilled Turbot	Pounded Flank Steak with Tomato Salsa	Grilled Chicken Shish Tanoak	Scrumptious Shrimp Scampi Fry
531st day	**532nd day**	**533rd day**	**534th day**	**535th day**	**536th day**	**537th day**	**538th day**	**539th day**	**540th day**
Easy Italian Frittata	Cheesy Broccoli-Rice Bake	Feta-Spinach 'n Pita Casserole	Chili and Yogurt Marinated Chicken	Air Fried Roasted Summer Squash	Grilled Potato Packets	Broiled Spiced-Lemon Squid	Strip Steak with Japanese Dipping Sauce	Sweetly Honeyed Chicken Kebabs	Salmon with Crisped Topped Crumbs
541st day	**542nd day**	**543rd day**	**544th day**	**545th day**	**546th day**	**547th day**	**548th day**	**549th day**	**550th day**
Breakfast Biscuits, Eggs 'n Bacon	Green Bean ' Chicken Stuffing Bake	Southwest Style Meaty Casserole	Grilled Chicken with Board Dressing	Grilled Cauliflower Bites	Grilled Sweet Onions	Tuna Grill with Ginger Sauce	Chi Spacca's Bistecca	Chicken and Pineapple BBQ	Baked Cod in Air Fryer
551st day	**552nd day**	**553rd day**	**554th day**	**555th day**	**556th day**	**557th day**	**558th day**	**559th day**	**560th day**
Hash Brown, Sausage 'n Cauliflower Bake	Yummy Mac 'n Cheese	Nutritious Cabbage Roll Bake	Indian Spiced Chicken Eggplant and Tomato Skewers	Roasted Air Fried Vegetables	Roasted Dill Potato Medley	Char-Grilled Spicy Halibut	Grilled Steak with Parsley Salad	Skewered Beef Asian Way	Orange-Caesar Dressed Roughie
561st day	**562nd day**	**563rd day**	**564th day**	**565th day**	**566th day**	**567th day**	**568th day**	**569th day**	**570th day**
Cauliflower-Broccoli Egg Bake	Mouth-Watering Taco Bake	Easy-Bake Spanish Rice	Easy Curry Grilled	Air Fryer Grilled	Grilled Squash	Roasted Swordfish with	Korean Grilled Skirt Steak	Chicken Kebabs Greek Way	Gouda-Spinach Stuffed Pork

			Chicken Wings	Mexican Corn		Charred Leeks			
571st day	572nd day	573rd day	574th day	575th day	576th day	577th day	578th day	579th day	580th day
Raisin 'n Apple French Toast	Rice Casserole Mexican Style	Brown Rice 'n Chicken Curry Casserole	Spicy Chicken with Lemon and Parsley in A Packet	Crispy and Spicy Grilled Broccoli in Air Fryer	Air Fryer Grilled Fennel	Citrusy Branzini on the Grill	Onion Marinated Skirt Steak	Skewered Oriental Teriyaki Beef	Buffalo Chicken Dip Bake
581st day	582nd day	583rd day	584th day	585th day	586th day	587th day	588th day	589th day	590th day
Overnight French Toast with Blueberries	Black Bean and Brown Rice Bake	Rotisserie Chicken with Herbes De Provence	Korean Grilled Chicken	Easy Grilled Corn in The Air Fryer	Grilled Corn Kabobs	Grilled Squid Rings with Kale and Tomatoes	Grilled Beef Steak with Herby Marinade	Grilled Beef with Ginger-Hoisin	Tender Chicken Thigh Bake
591st day	592nd day	593rd day	594th day	595th day	596th day	597th day	598th day	599th day	600th day
Eggs Benedict in an Overnight Casserole	Herb and Zucchini Bake	Grilled Oregano Chicken	Grilled Chicken with Shishito Peppers	Grilled Pineapple and Peppers	Grill Smoked Mushrooms	Butterflied Sriracha Prawns Grilled	Crunchy Crisped Peaches	Spiced Lime 'n Coconut Shrimp Skewer	Chicken Teriyaki Bake
601st day	602nd day	603rd day	604th day	605th day	606th day	607th day	608th day	609th day	610th day
Egg-Substitute 'n Bacon Casserole	A Different Rice-Chik'n Bake	Honey Sriracha Chicken	Grilled Chicken with Scallions	Grilled Onion Potatoes	Blackened Shrimps in Air Fryer	Grilled Shrimp with Butter	Five-Cheese Pull Apart Bread	Teriyaki 'n Hawaiian Chicken	Meatball Pizza Bake
611th day	612th day	613th day	614th day	615th day	616th day	617th day	618th day	619th day	620th day
Country style Brekky Casserole	Sea Scallop Bake	Tequila Glazed Chicken	Piri Piri Chicken	Grilled Frozen Vegetables	Herb and Garlic Fish Fingers	Char-Grilled 'n Herbed Sea Scallops	Buttery Dinner Rolls	Tangy Grilled Fig-Prosciutto	Pepperoni Calzone Bake
621st day	622nd day	623rd day	624th day	625th day	626th day	627th day	628th day	629th day	630th day
Amish Style Brekky Casserole	Portuguese Bacalao Tapas	Grilled Sambal Chicken	Grilled Turmeric and Lemongrass Chicken	Simple Grilled Vegetables	Crispy Cod Nuggets with Tartar Sauce	Japanese Citrus Soy Squid	Yummy Carrot Cake	Veggie Souvlaki on Air Fryer Grill	Comforting Beef Stew Bake
631st day	632nd day	633rd day	634th day	635th day	636th day	637th day	638th day	639th day	640th day
Baked Cornbread and Eggs	Shrimp Casserole Louisiana Style	Smoked Chicken Wings	Peruvian Grilled Chicken	Italian Grilled Vegetables	Garlic and Black Pepper Shrimp Grill	Greek-Style Grilled Scallops	Tangy Orange-Chococake	Swordfish with Sage on the Grill	Roll-up Chicken Reuben

641st day	642nd day	643rd day	644th day	645th day	646th day	647th day	648th day	649th day	650th day
Feta and Spinach Brekky Pie	Lobster Lasagna Maine Style	Sweet and Sour Grilled Chicken	Air Fryer Grilled Moroccan Chicken	Balsamic Grilled Vegetables	Grilled Salmon with Cucumbers	Easy Grilled Pesto Scallops	Delightful Caramel Cheesecake	Scallops and Bacon Grill	Chicken Mediterranean Fry
651st day	652nd day	653rd day	654th day	655th day	656th day	657th day	658th day	659th day	660th day
Cheesy-Bacon Casserole	Rice and Tuna Puff	Lemon Grilled Chicken Breasts	Rotisserie Chicken with Herbes De Provence	Grilled Vegetables with Lemon Herb Vinaigrette	Shrimps, Zucchini, And Tomatoes on the Grill	Clams with Herbed Butter in Packets	Amazing with Every Bite Fried Bananas	Grilled Chipotle Shrimp	3-Cheese Meatball Bake
661st day	662nd day	663rd day	664th day	665th day	666th day	667th day	668th day	669th day	670th day
Mixed Vegetable Frittata	Cheesy Zucchini-Squash Bake	Spicy Peach Glazed Grilled Chicken	Grilled Oregano Chicken	Grilled Vegetables with Garlic	Grilled Halibut with Tomatoes and Hearts of Palm	Simple Sesame Squid on the Grill	Sugared Doughs with Choco Dip	Dill-Rubbed Grilled Salmon	Crusted Fish with Dijon
671st day	672nd day	673rd day	674th day	675th day	676th day	677th day	678th day	679th day	680th day
Breakfast Chicken Casserole	Yellow Squash Bake, Low Carb	Chinese Style Chicken	Honey Sriracha Chicken	Grilled Asparagus with Hollandaise Sauce	Chat Masala Grilled Snapper	Grilled Shellfish with Vegetables	Enchanting Coffee-Apple Cake	Turkey Meatballs in Skewer	Rosemary Pork with Apricot Glaze
681st day	682nd day	683rd day	684th day	685th day	686th day	687th day	688th day	689th day	690th day
Rice Casserole Mexican Style	Zucchini & Carrot Bake	Garlic Cilantro-Lime Chicken	Tequila Glazed Chicken	Grilled Zucchini with Mozzarella	One-Pan Shrimp and Chorizo Mix Grill	Grilled Meat Recipes	Pumpkin Pie in Air Fryer	Grilled Curried Chicken	Tater Tot, Cheeseburger 'n Bacon Bake
691st day	692nd day	693rd day	694th day	695th day	696th day	697th day	698th day	699th day	700th day
Broccoli, Ham 'n Potato Casserole	Cheesy-Creamy Broccoli Bake	Grilled Chicken Stuffed with Cheese	Grilled Sambal Chicken	Grilled Tomato Melts	Grilled Tasty Scallops	Sous Vide Smoked Brisket	Blackberry-Goodness Cobbler	Chicken Caesar on the Grill	Chicago-Style Deep Dish Pizza
701st day	702nd day	703rd day	704th day	705th day	706th day	707th day	708th day	709th day	710th day
Cheeseburger and Bacon Casserole	Mushroom 'n Spinach Casserole	Southwest Chicken Foil Packets	Smoked Chicken Wings	Grilled Asparagus and Arugula Salad	Clam with Lemons on the Grill	Skirt Steak with Mojo Marinade	Appetizing Apple Pound Cake	Grilled Jerk Chicken	Creamy Coconut Sauce on Jamaican Salmon
711th day	712th day	713th day	714th day	715th day	716th day	717th day	718th day	719th day	720th day

Vegan Approved Shepherd's Pie	Potato Casserole Twice Baked	Teriyaki Grilled Chicken	Sweet and Sour Grilled Chicken	Air Fryer Grilled Mushrooms	Salmon Steak Grilled with Cilantro Garlic Sauce	Dijon-Marinated Skirt Steak	Cranberry Bread Pudding	Rosemary-Rubbed Grilled Lamb	Chicken Bruschetta Bake
721st day	722nd day	723rd day	724th day	725th day	726th day	727th day	728th day	729th day	730th day
Enchilada Leftovers Casserole	Chicken Deluxe Tetrazzini	Sweet and Spicy Grilled Chicken	Lemon Grilled Chicken Breasts	Spicy Thai – Style Veggies	Tasty Grilled Red Mullet	Grilled Carne Asada Steak	Easy 'n Delicious Brownies	Thai-Style Grilled Pork	Turkey 'n Biscuit Bake
731st day	732nd day	733rd day	734th day	735th day	736th day	737th day	738th day	739th day	740th day
Rice, Chicken 'n Salsa Casserole	Chili Rellenos Bake	Hone, Lime, And Lime Grilled Chicken	Spicy Peach Glazed Grilled Chicken	Grilled Vegetables with Smokey Mustard Sauce	Chargrilled Halibut Niçoise With Vegetables	Chimichurri-Style Steak	Luscious Strawberry Cobbler	Cajun Pork on the Grill	Amazingly Healthy Zucchini Bake
741st day	742nd day	743rd day	744th day	745th day	746th day	747th day	748th day	749th day	750th day
Turkey 'n Broccoli Bake	Spicy Zucchini Bake Mexican Style	Grilled Jerk Chicken	Chinese Style Chicken	Indian Grilled Vegetables	Spiced Salmon Kebabs	Strip Steak with Cucumber Yogurt Sauce	Sour Cream-Blueberry Coffee Cake	Grilled Buccaneer Pork	Grilled Frozen Vegetables
751st day	752nd day	753rd day	754th day	755th day	756th day	757th day	758th day	759th day	760th day
Creamy Broccoli Egg Scramble	Veggie-Pasta 'n chicken Bake	Eggplant-Parm Bake	Butterflied Chicken with Herbs	Air Fried Grilled Asparagus	Grilled Sweet Potato Wedges with Dipping Sauce	Roasted Tuna on Linguine	Grilled BBQ Sausages	Appealingly Coconut-y Cake	Hungarian Style Grilled Beef
761st day	762nd day	763rd day	764th day	765th day	766th day	767th day	768th day	769th day	770th day
Loaded Breakfast Hash Browns	Penne Chicken Pesto Bake	Seven Layers of Tortilla Pie	4-Ingredient Garlic Herb Chicken Wings	Grilled Hasselback Potatoes	Grilled Green Beans with Shallots	Chili Lime Clams with Tomatoes	Medium Rare Simple Salt and Pepper Steak	Beef Eastern Shish Kebabs	Orange & Tofu Fry
771st day	772nd day	773rd day	774th day	775th day	776th day	777th day	778th day	779th day	780th day
Biscuit, Sausage 'n Egg Layer Casserole	Chicken Florentine Bake	Penne Pasta 'n Portobello Bake	Pesto Grilled Chicken	Air Fryer Roasted Vegetables	Grille Tomatoes with Garden Herb Salad	Air Fryer Garlicky-Grilled Turbot	Pounded Flank Steak with Tomato Salsa	Grilled Chicken Shish Tanoak	Scrumptious Shrimp Scampi Fry
781st day	782nd day	783rd day	784th day	785th day	786th day	787th day	788th day	789th day	790th day

Easy Italian Frittata	Cheesy Broccoli-Rice Bake	Feta-Spinach 'n Pita Casserole	Chili and Yogurt Marinated Chicken	Air Fried Roasted Summer Squash	Grilled Potato Packets	Broiled Spiced-Lemon Squid	Strip Steak with Japanese Dipping Sauce	Sweetly Honeyed Chicken Kebabs	Salmon with Crisped Topped Crumbs
791st day	**792nd day**	**793rd day**	**794th day**	**795th day**	**796th day**	**797th day**	**798th day**	**799th day**	**800th day**
Breakfast Biscuits, Eggs 'n Bacon	Green Bean ' Chicken Stuffing Bake	Southwest Style Meaty Casserole	Grilled Chicken with Board Dressing	Grilled Cauliflower Bites	Grilled Sweet Onions	Tuna Grill with Ginger Sauce	Chi Spacca's Bistecca	Chicken and Pineapple BBQ	Baked Cod in Air Fryer
801st day	**802nd day**	**803rd day**	**804th day**	**805th day**	**806th day**	**807th day**	**808th day**	**809th day**	**810th day**
Hash Brown, Sausage 'n Cauliflower Bake	Yummy Mac 'n Cheese	Nutritious Cabbage Roll Bake	Indian Spiced Chicken Eggplant and Tomato Skewers	Roasted Air Fried Vegetables	Roasted Dill Potato Medley	Char-Grilled Spicy Halibut	Grilled Steak with Parsley Salad	Skewered Beef Asian Way	Orange-Caesar Dressed Roughie
811th day	**812th day**	**813th day**	**814th day**	**815th day**	**816th day**	**817th day**	**818th day**	**819th day**	**820th day**
Cauliflower-Broccoli Egg Bake	Mouth-Watering Taco Bake	Easy-Bake Spanish Rice	Easy Curry Grilled Chicken Wings	Air Fryer Grilled Mexican Corn	Grilled Squash	Roasted Swordfish with Charred Leeks	Korean Grilled Skirt Steak	Chicken Kebabs Greek Way	Gouda-Spinach Stuffed Pork
821st day	**822nd day**	**823rd day**	**824th day**	**825th day**	**826th day**	**827th day**	**828th day**	**829th day**	**830th day**
Raisin 'n Apple French Toast	Rice Casserole Mexican Style	Brown Rice 'n Chicken Curry Casserole	Spicy Chicken with Lemon and Parsley in A Packet	Crispy and Spicy Grilled Broccoli in Air Fryer	Air Fryer Grilled Fennel	Citrusy Branzini on the Grill	Onion Marinated Skirt Steak	Skewered Oriental Teriyaki Beef	Buffalo Chicken Dip Bake
831st day	**832nd day**	**833rd day**	**834th day**	**835th day**	**836th day**	**837th day**	**838th day**	**839th day**	**840th day**
Overnight French Toast with Blueberries	Black Bean and Brown Rice Bake	Rotisserie Chicken with Herbes De Provence	Korean Grilled Chicken	Easy Grilled Corn in The Air Fryer	Grilled Corn Kabobs	Grilled Squid Rings with Kale and Tomatoes	Grilled Beef Steak with Herby Marinade	Grilled Beef with Ginger-Hoisin	Tender Chicken Thigh Bake
841st day	**842nd day**	**843rd day**	**844th day**	**845th day**	**846th day**	**847th day**	**848th day**	**849th day**	**850th day**
Eggs Benedict in an Overnight Casserole	Herb and Zucchini Bake	Grilled Oregano Chicken	Grilled Chicken with Shishito Peppers	Grilled Pineapple and Peppers	Grill Smoked Mushrooms	Butterflied Sriracha Prawns Grilled	Crunchy Crisped Peaches	Spiced Lime 'n Coconut Shrimp Skewer	Chicken Teriyaki Bake
851st day	**852nd day**	**853rd day**	**854th day**	**855th day**	**856th day**	**857th day**	**858th day**	**859th day**	**860th day**

Egg-Substitute 'n Bacon Casserole	A Different Rice-Chik'n Bake	Honey Sriracha Chicken	Grilled Chicken with Scallions	Grilled Onion Potatoes	Blackened Shrimps in Air Fryer	Grilled Shrimp with Butter	Five-Cheese Pull Apart Bread	Teriyaki 'n Hawaiian Chicken	Meatball Pizza Bake
861st day	**862nd day**	**863rd day**	**864th day**	**865th day**	**866th day**	**867th day**	**868th day**	**869th day**	**870th day**
Country style Brekky Casserole	Sea Scallop Bake	Tequila Glazed Chicken	Piri Piri Chicken	Grilled Frozen Vegetables	Herb and Garlic Fish Fingers	Char-Grilled 'n Herbed Sea Scallops	Buttery Dinner Rolls	Tangy Grilled Fig-Prosciutto	Pepperoni Calzone Bake
871st day	**872nd day**	**873rd day**	**874th day**	**875th day**	**876th day**	**877th day**	**878th day**	**879th day**	**880th day**
Amish Style Brekky Casserole	Portuguese Bacalao Tapas	Grilled Sambal Chicken	Grilled Turmeric and Lemongrass Chicken	Simple Grilled Vegetables	Crispy Cod Nuggets with Tartar Sauce	Japanese Citrus Soy Squid	Yummy Carrot Cake	Veggie Souvlaki on Air Fryer Grill	Comforting Beef Stew Bake
881st day	**882nd day**	**883rd day**	**884th day**	**885th day**	**886th day**	**887th day**	**888th day**	**889th day**	**890th day**
Baked Cornbread and Eggs	Shrimp Casserole Louisiana Style	Smoked Chicken Wings	Peruvian Grilled Chicken	Italian Grilled Vegetables	Garlic and Black Pepper Shrimp Grill	Greek-Style Grilled Scallops	Tangy Orange-Choco cake	Swordfish with Sage on the Grill	Roll-up Chicken Reuben
891st day	**892nd day**	**893rd day**	**894th day**	**895th day**	**896th day**	**897th day**	**898th day**	**899th day**	**900th day**
Feta and Spinach Brekky Pie	Lobster Lasagna Maine Style	Sweet and Sour Grilled Chicken	Air Fryer Grilled Moroccan Chicken	Balsamic Grilled Vegetables	Grilled Salmon with Cucumbers	Easy Grilled Pesto Scallops	Delightful Caramel Cheesecake	Scallops and Bacon Grill	Chicken Mediterranean Fry
901st day	**902nd day**	**903rd day**	**904th day**	**905th day**	**906th day**	**907th day**	**908th day**	**909th day**	**910th day**
Cheesy-Bacon Casserole	Rice and Tuna Puff	Lemon Grilled Chicken	Rotisserie Chicken with Herbes De Provence	Grilled Vegetables with Lemon Herb Vinaigrette	Shrimps, Zucchini, And Tomatoes on the Grill	Clams with Herbed Butter in Packets	Amazing with Every Bite Fried Bananas	Grilled Chipotle Shrimp	3-Cheese Meatball Bake
911th day	**912th day**	**913th day**	**914th day**	**915th day**	**916th day**	**917th day**	**918th day**	**919th day**	**920th day**
Mixed Vegetable Frittata	Cheesy Zucchini-Squash Bake	Spicy Peach Glazed Grilled Chicken	Grilled Oregano Chicken	Grilled Vegetables with Garlic	Grilled Halibut with Tomatoes and Hearts of Palm	Simple Sesame Squid on the Grill	Sugared Doughs with Choco Dip	Dill-Rubbed Grilled Salmon	Crusted Fish with Dijon
921st day	**922nd day**	**923rd day**	**924th day**	**925th day**	**926th day**	**927th day**	**928th day**	**929th day**	**930th day**
Breakfast Chicken Casserole	Yellow Squash Bake, Low Carb	Chinese Style Chicken	Honey Sriracha Chicken	Grilled Asparagus with Holland	Chat Masala Grilled Snapper	Grilled Shellfish with Vegetables	Enchanting Coffee-Apple Cake	Turkey Meatballs in Skewer	Rosemary Pork with Apricot Glaze

931st day	932nd day	933rd day	934th day	935th day	936th day	937th day	938th day	939th day	940th day
Rice Casserole Mexican Style	Zucchini & Carrot Bake	Garlic Cilantro-Lime Chicken	Tequila Glazed Chicken	Grilled Zucchini with Mozzarella	One-Pan Shrimp and Chorizo Mix Grill	Grilled Meat Recipes	Pumpkin Pie in Air Fryer	Grilled Curried Chicken	Tater Tot, Cheeseburger 'n Bacon Bake
941st day	942nd day	943rd day	944th day	945th day	946th day	947th day	948th day	949th day	950th day
Broccoli, Ham 'n Potato Casserole	Cheesy-Creamy Broccoli Bake	Grilled Chicken Stuffed with Cheese	Grilled Sambal Chicken	Grilled Tomato Melts	Grilled Tasty Scallops	Sous Vide Smoked Brisket	Blackberry-Goodness Cobbler	Chicken Caesar on the Grill	Chicago-Style Deep Dish Pizza
951st day	952nd day	953rd day	954th day	955th day	956th day	957th day	958th day	959th day	960th day
Cheeseburger and Bacon Casserole	Mushroom 'n Spinach Casserole	Southwest Chicken Foil Packets	Smoked Chicken Wings	Grilled Asparagus and Arugula Salad	Clam with Lemons on the Grill	Skirt Steak with Mojo Marinade	Appetizing Apple Pound Cake	Grilled Jerk Chicken	Creamy Coconut Sauce on Jamaican Salmon
961st day	962nd day	963rd day	964th day	965th day	966th day	967th day	968th day	969th day	970th day
Vegan Approved Shepherd's Pie	Potato Casserole Twice Baked	Teriyaki Grilled Chicken	Sweet and Sour Grilled Chicken	Air Fryer Grilled Mushrooms	Salmon Steak Grilled with Cilantro Garlic Sauce	Dijon-Marinated Skirt Steak	Cranberry Bread Pudding	Rosemary-Rubbed Grilled Lamb	Chicken Bruschetta Bake
971st day	972nd day	973rd day	974th day	975th day	976th day	977th day	978th day	979th day	980th day
Enchilada Leftovers Casserole	Chicken Deluxe Tetrazzini	Sweet and Spicy Grilled Chicken	Lemon Grilled Chicken Breasts	Spicy Thai – Style Veggies	Tasty Grilled Red Mullet	Grilled Carne Asada Steak	Easy 'n Delicious Brownies	Thai-Style Grilled Pork	Turkey 'n Biscuit Bake
981st day	982nd day	983rd day	984th day	985th day	986th day	987th day	988th day	989th day	990th day
Rice, Chicken 'n Salsa Casserole	Chili Rellenos Bake	Hone, Lime, And Lime Grilled Chicken	Spicy Peach Glazed Grilled Chicken	Grilled Vegetables with Smokey Mustard Sauce	Chargrilled Halibut Niçoise With Vegetables	Chimichurri-Style Steak	Luscious Strawberry Cobbler	Cajun Pork on the Grill	Amazingly Healthy Zucchini Bake
991st day	992nd day	993rd day	994th day	995th day	996th day	997th day	998th day	999th day	1000th day
Turkey 'n Broccoli Bake	Spicy Zucchini Bake Mexican Style	Grilled Jerk Chicken	Chinese Style Chicken	Indian Grilled Vegetables	Spiced Salmon Kebabs	Strip Steak with Cucumb	Sour Cream-Blueberry	Grilled Buccaneer Pork	Grilled Frozen Vegetables

| | | | | | er Yogurt Sauce | Coffee Cake | | |

Made in the USA
Middletown, DE
06 March 2019